REPTILE AND AMPHIBIAN CARE GUIDE

Balancing Human Passion with Animal
Welfare: Best Practices in Herpetological
Care and Ethical Responsibility

By

KAREN G. LEMON

3

Table of contents

5

Introduction

Reptiles and amphibians have fascinated humans for centuries. From the patient stillness of a tortoise to the vibrant calls of tree frogs, these creatures embody some of the most ancient and resilient lineages on Earth. Today, they are increasingly kept as companions, offering a window into the natural world and an opportunity to connect with life far removed from the familiar mammal and bird pets.

This guide was created to provide both new and experienced keepers with a **comprehensive resource for reptile and amphibian husbandry**. Covering topics from species selection and enclosure design to veterinary care, breeding, enrichment, and ethics, it seeks to balance practical instruction with respect for the animals themselves.

Above all, it emphasizes that keeping reptiles and amphibians is not simply about maintaining pets—it is about becoming a **guardian of ancient life**

forms whose wellbeing depends entirely on human stewardship. By learning and applying best practices, keepers not only improve the lives of their animals but also contribute to global efforts in conservation, education, and appreciation of biodiversity.

Chapter 1

Introduction To Reptiles And Amphibians

1.1 Understanding the Appeal of Reptiles and Amphibians

Reptiles and amphibians—often grouped together under the term *herpetofauna*—represent some of the most fascinating animals on Earth. From the jewel-toned poison dart frog of South America to the slow-moving tortoise of the African savannah, these creatures embody remarkable adaptations that allow them to thrive in diverse environments. Unlike traditional companion animals such as cats and dogs, reptiles and amphibians provide owners with an entirely different perspective on animal care: one that emphasizes habitat replication, respect for natural behaviors, and a deeper appreciation of ecological systems.

For many enthusiasts, the allure lies in their uniqueness. They move, eat, and interact in ways very different from mammals and birds. They are ancient survivors, tracing their evolutionary roots back hundreds of millions of years. Keeping one of these animals in captivity is not only an exercise in pet care but also an opportunity to witness living history unfold inside a terrarium.

However, this fascination must be balanced with responsibility. Too often, reptiles and amphibians are acquired impulsively, with little understanding of their needs. Unlike more domesticated species, these animals require specialized environments and precise conditions to thrive. A lack of preparation can quickly lead to stress, illness, or premature death. This guide begins, therefore, with a strong emphasis on education, ensuring that readers understand the profound responsibility that comes with keeping reptiles and amphibians as companions.

1.2 Defining Reptiles and Amphibians

Before diving deeper into care, it is essential to clarify what distinguishes reptiles and amphibians. Though they are often lumped together in the pet trade and in common conversation, they are biologically distinct groups.

Reptiles are cold-blooded vertebrates covered in scales or scutes. They include turtles and tortoises, snakes, lizards, and crocodilians. Their dry, keratinized skin reduces water loss, allowing them to thrive in environments that range from arid deserts to lush tropical forests. Most reptiles lay eggs with leathery shells, though some species give birth to live young.

Amphibians, on the other hand, include frogs, toads, salamanders, and caecilians. They are unique in that they often experience *metamorphosis*—starting life in an aquatic, gilled larval stage and transforming into a more terrestrial adult form. Their permeable skin makes them highly sensitive to environmental changes, particularly humidity, water quality, and toxins. Unlike reptiles, amphibians rely heavily on moisture to survive, and many must remain in damp conditions throughout their lives.

Together, reptiles and amphibians provide a window into evolutionary biology, showing us how life has adapted to land, water, and the transitional spaces in between.

1.3 Historical and Cultural Significance

Reptiles and amphibians have held symbolic significance across cultures and eras. In ancient Egypt, the crocodile was revered and feared, associated with the god Sobek. Snakes appear in mythology across the world: as healers in the Greek symbol of Asclepius, as tempters in Judeo-Christian tradition, and as symbols of rebirth in countless cultures due to their ability to shed their skin.

Amphibians, too, have fascinated humans. Frogs often represent fertility and transformation due to their dual life cycle. In Mesoamerican cultures, the axolotl was considered sacred and associated with the god Xolotl, embodying resilience and regeneration.

In modern times, reptiles and amphibians have moved from mythological icons to beloved pets, research animals, and ambassadors for conservation. Their cultural journey highlights humanity's evolving relationship with the natural world.

1.4 Common Misconceptions

Before delving into care, it is crucial to dispel several misconceptions that often lead to neglect or mistreatment:

1. **"Reptiles and amphibians are low-maintenance pets."**
   In reality, while they may not require daily walks or constant companionship, they demand carefully regulated environments. Heat, humidity, lighting, and diet must be monitored with precision.

2. **"They don't bond with humans."**
   Although they do not form attachments in the same way as mammals, many reptiles can recognize their keepers, learn feeding routines, and exhibit calmness when handled correctly.

3. **"Small reptiles are easy to keep."**
   Size does not determine difficulty. Some small species, like dart frogs, require highly specialized diets and environments. Conversely, a larger

tortoise may have simpler needs but require immense space.

4. **"They can live in any tank."**
   Improper enclosures are one of the leading causes of premature death. Each species has specific requirements tied to its natural habitat that must be replicated as closely as possible.

By confronting these myths early, prospective keepers can enter the world of herpetology with realistic expectations.

1.5   Ethical   Considerations   of   Keeping Herpetofauna

The reptile and amphibian pet trade has grown rapidly over the past few decades, raising questions about conservation, welfare, and sustainability. While captive breeding has reduced the pressure on wild populations for some species, illegal collection and habitat destruction remain serious concerns.

Responsible keepers must ask themselves:

- Is this animal captive-bred or wild-caught?

- What is the long-term commitment required, and am I prepared to meet it?

- If I can no longer provide care, what are the rehoming options?

These questions highlight the ethical weight of ownership. Unlike short-lived pets, some tortoises may live well over 70 years, requiring generational planning for their care. Amphibians, though often shorter-lived, demand careful attention due to their sensitivity to environmental changes and their role as ecological indicators.

Keeping reptiles and amphibians is therefore not merely a hobby—it is a stewardship responsibility that connects the keeper to broader issues of biodiversity and conservation.

1.6 The Role of Reptiles and Amphibians in Ecosystems

Another dimension of understanding these animals lies in recognizing their ecological importance. Both reptiles and amphibians occupy crucial niches:

- **Predators of pests**: Frogs and toads consume vast quantities of insects, reducing mosquito populations and controlling agricultural pests.

- **Prey for larger animals**: They form an integral part of the food web, feeding birds, mammals, and fish.

- **Ecosystem indicators**: Amphibians, due to their permeable skin, serve as early warning systems for environmental decline. Their decline in many regions signals habitat destruction, pollution, or climate change.

For keepers, appreciating their ecological roles reinforces the importance of responsible care. A reptile or amphibian in captivity is not just a pet but also an ambassador for its species and ecosystem.

1.7 Reptiles and Amphibians as Educational Tools

Beyond companionship, reptiles and amphibians serve as powerful educational tools. In classrooms, zoos, and nature centers, they spark curiosity in children and adults alike. Observing a snake shed its skin or a frog metamorphose from tadpole to adult fosters a tangible understanding of biology.

For many young enthusiasts, their first reptile—perhaps a leopard gecko or corn snake—becomes a gateway to a lifelong passion for science, conservation, or veterinary medicine. Their care demands attention to detail, patience, and respect, qualities that transfer to other aspects of life.

1.8 Preparing for Ownership

Given the complexities outlined, preparation is paramount. Before acquiring a reptile or amphibian, prospective owners should:

1. **Research thoroughly**: Understand the species' habitat, diet, behavior, and lifespan.

2. **Invest in proper equipment**: Quality enclosures, heating systems, and lighting are non-negotiable.

3. **Budget realistically**: Veterinary care, food, and habitat maintenance can add up.

4. **Commit for the long term**: Many reptiles live decades, requiring stable care and planning.

Ownership begins not with purchase, but with preparation. A well-prepared keeper creates conditions for success, while an unprepared one risks the animal's health and welfare.

1.9 The Keeper's Role in Conservation and Awareness

Every reptile or amphibian keeper plays a role in shaping public perception. Responsible care practices not only improve animal welfare but also combat stereotypes of reptiles as "dangerous," "ugly," or "disposable."

Engaged keepers often find themselves drawn into conservation initiatives—whether supporting captive breeding programs, educating the public, or advocating against illegal wildlife trade. By keeping these animals with respect and care, owners become informal ambassadors for biodiversity.

1.10 Conclusion: A Journey of Respect and Responsibility

This introduction underscores a central theme: keeping reptiles and amphibians is a privilege that demands knowledge, patience, and respect. These are not animals to be acquired on impulse but living beings with complex needs and ecological significance.

As this guide unfolds in subsequent chapters, readers will gain the tools to choose appropriate species, design enclosures that mimic natural habitats, provide proper nutrition, and ensure long-term health and well-being.

Ultimately, the decision to bring a reptile or amphibian into one's life is the start of a journey—one that connects the keeper not only to their animal but also to a broader web of history, culture, and conservation. By embracing this journey with care and responsibility, one can experience the profound joy of sharing life with some of nature's most remarkable survivors.

Chapter 2

Choosing the Right Species

2.1 The Importance Of Careful Selection

One of the most critical decisions in reptile and amphibian keeping is the choice of species. Unlike traditional pets, where basic needs such as food, exercise, and companionship remain relatively consistent, reptiles and amphibians display vast differences in requirements. An animal's size, temperament, dietary needs, environmental conditions, and lifespan all play determining roles in its suitability for a given keeper.

Too often, people acquire these animals based on impulse— drawn to the striking colors of a dart frog, the intimidating appearance of a large python, or the slow charm of a tortoise—without understanding the level of commitment involved. Unfortunately, this mismatch between desire and practicality often results in poor welfare outcomes for the animal and disillusionment for the owner.

This chapter provides a structured framework for evaluating and choosing the right species, ensuring both the keeper and the animal can enjoy a sustainable, fulfilling relationship.

2.2 Factors to Consider Before Choosing a Species

1. Experience Level of the Keeper

- **Beginner-Friendly Species**: Some reptiles and amphibians are hardy, adaptable, and forgiving of minor mistakes. These are best suited for first-time keepers. Examples include leopard geckos, corn snakes, and African dwarf frogs.

- **Intermediate Species**: These animals may require more precise environmental control, specialized diets, or greater handling care. Examples include ball pythons, bearded dragons, and fire-bellied toads.

- **Advanced Species**: Reserved for highly experienced keepers, these animals may be large, dangerous, delicate, or require highly specialized enclosures. Examples include monitor lizards, green tree pythons, and poison dart frogs.

2.   Lifespan   and   Long-Term   Commitment
Reptiles and amphibians vary enormously in longevity:

- Small frogs may live 5–10 years.

- Corn snakes and leopard geckos can live 15–20 years.

- Tortoises can live 50–100 years or more, often outliving their owners.
  Lifespan is a crucial factor; an animal should never be viewed as a temporary curiosity.

3.   Space   Requirements
An animal's adult size dictates enclosure needs. A hatchling iguana may fit in a small terrarium but can grow to over 6 feet, requiring a room-sized enclosure. Conversely, dart frogs remain small but need elaborate vertical habitats with live plants and careful humidity control.

4. Diet and Feeding Requirements

- **Insectivores** (e.g., leopard geckos, tree frogs) require regular access to live feeder insects.

- **Carnivores** (e.g., snakes, monitor lizards) may need pre-killed rodents or fish.

- **Herbivores** (e.g., iguanas, tortoises) depend on a constant supply of fresh greens and vegetables.

- **Specialists** (e.g., horned lizards that feed almost exclusively on ants) can be nearly impossible to maintain in captivity.

5.   Handling   and   Temperament
Some species tolerate gentle handling, while others become stressed or aggressive when touched. If interaction is important, species like bearded dragons or corn snakes are better suited than dart frogs or chameleons, which should rarely be handled.

6.   Cost   of   Ownership
The purchase price of the animal is often only a fraction of the expense. Enclosures, lighting, heating, food, supplements, and veterinary care may far exceed the cost of the animal itself. A realistic budget is essential.

7.   Legal   and   Ethical   Considerations
Many regions regulate or prohibit certain species, particularly venomous snakes, large constrictors, crocodilians, or endangered amphibians. Always check local regulations, and ensure that the animal comes from a reputable, legal source.

2.3 Beginner-Friendly Species Recommendations

For newcomers to herpetology, certain reptiles and amphibians have proven themselves reliable, resilient, and relatively simple to maintain.

Reptiles:

- **Leopard Gecko (Eublepharis macularius)**: Hardy, small, requires moderate space, insectivorous diet, and is generally docile.

- **Corn Snake (Pantherophis guttatus)**: Non-venomous, easy to handle, readily available in captive-bred morphs, and feeds on pre-killed rodents.

- **Bearded Dragon (Pogona vitticeps)**: Interactive, hardy, enjoys basking and moderate handling, requires a larger enclosure but makes an excellent display animal.

Amphibians:

- **African Dwarf Frog (Hymenochirus spp.)**: Fully aquatic, easy to maintain in an aquarium, small size, and relatively hardy.

- **White's Tree Frog (Ranoidea caerulea)**: Docile, adaptable, tolerant of beginner mistakes, and often lives 15 years in captivity.

- **Fire-Bellied Toad (Bombina orientalis)**: Hardy and visually striking, requiring a simple semi-aquatic setup.

2.4 Intermediate Species for Dedicated Keepers

Once basic husbandry skills are mastered, intermediate species can provide more challenges and rewards.

Reptiles:

- **Ball Python (Python regius)**: Popular and relatively gentle, but requires precise humidity and temperature control.

- **Blue-Tongued Skink (Tiliqua spp.)**: Intelligent, omnivorous diet, and can become quite personable.

- **Uromastyx (Uromastyx spp.)**: Herbivorous desert lizard, requires high heat and UVB exposure.

Amphibians:

- **Axolotl (Ambystoma mexicanum)**: Aquatic, fascinating regenerative abilities, requires cool, pristine water conditions.

- **Pacman Frog (Ceratophrys spp.)**: Voracious appetite, sedentary, requires careful humidity maintenance.

- **Tiger Salamander (Ambystoma tigrinum)**: Hardy but requires a moist terrestrial setup with burrowing substrate.

2.5 Advanced and Specialist Species

Advanced species are best left to experienced enthusiasts due to their size, danger, or delicate needs.

Reptiles:

- **Green Iguana (Iguana iguana)**: Attractive but can grow over six feet, requiring enormous space and strict diet.

- **Monitor Lizards (Varanus spp.)**: Intelligent, powerful, and often aggressive; require advanced enclosures and large prey.

- **Green Tree Python (Morelia viridis)**: Striking coloration, but highly sensitive to humidity and stress.

Amphibians:

- **Poison Dart Frogs (Dendrobates spp.)**:
  Brilliantly colored and captivating, but demand
  precise humidity, diet, and live plant setups.

- **Caecilians (Gymnophiona)**: Rare in captivity,
  secretive burrowers, and difficult to maintain.

- **Glass Frogs (Centrolenidae)**: Require delicate,
  humid rainforest environments and are extremely
  sensitive to stress.

2.6 Common Mistakes in Species Selection

- **Underestimating Size**: Many keepers purchase
  baby reptiles without realizing their full adult size
  (e.g., Burmese pythons).

- **Ignoring Lifespan**: A tortoise living over 70
  years requires generational planning.

- **Impulse Purchases**: Choosing based on
  appearance rather than practicality often leads to
  surrender or neglect.

- **Overestimating Handling Tolerance**:
  Amphibians, for example, often cannot tolerate

frequent handling due to delicate skin.

- **Inadequate Research**: Failing to study husbandry requirements before purchase is the most common mistake.

2.7 The Role of Captive Breeding

Whenever possible, prospective owners should choose **captive-bred** animals rather than wild-caught. Captive-bred animals are:

- More likely to be disease-free.

- Better acclimated to captivity.

- Less likely to carry parasites.

- Ethically preferable, reducing pressure on wild populations.

Wild-caught animals may appear cheaper but often come with hidden costs in terms of stress, illness, and mortality. Supporting reputable breeders and sellers helps promote sustainable practices within the herpetological community.

2.8 Matching Keeper Lifestyle with Animal Needs

Choosing the right species is not only about the animal but also about the keeper's lifestyle:

- **Busy schedules**: Species with less demanding daily care, such as corn snakes, may be suitable.

- **Hands-on interaction desired**: Bearded dragons or blue-tongued skinks often enjoy handling.

- **Limited space**: Smaller geckos or frogs are better suited than iguanas or tortoises.

- **Budget constraints**: Hardy, inexpensive species should be prioritized over delicate, high-maintenance animals.

A realistic assessment of one's time, budget, and expectations ensures a healthy balance between animal welfare and keeper satisfaction.

2.9 Ethical Responsibility in Species Choice

Beyond personal preference, choosing the right species carries broader ethical implications. Owning an animal that grows too large, proves dangerous, or has needs impossible to meet in captivity is not responsible stewardship. Likewise, keeping species that contribute to invasive populations if released (such as certain turtles and snakes) must be avoided.

Responsible ownership starts with saying "no" to species that cannot be provided for adequately.

2.10 Conclusion: Choosing with Care and Commitment

Selecting a reptile or amphibian is not merely about aesthetics or novelty—it is about compatibility, responsibility, and long-term commitment. The right choice balances the needs of the animal with the capabilities of the keeper, ensuring both can thrive together.

For beginners, hardy and forgiving species provide a safe introduction. For those seeking challenges, intermediate and advanced species offer rewarding experiences but require skill, dedication, and resources. Above all, ethical considerations, ecological responsibility, and realistic planning must guide every decision.

Choosing wisely lays the foundation for everything that follows: proper housing, diet, health, and enrichment. It is the single most important step in beginning the journey of reptile and amphibian care.

Chapter 3

Understanding Natural Habitats

3.1 Why Natural Habitats Matter in Captive Care

For reptiles and amphibians, survival depends heavily on the environment. Unlike mammals, which generate and regulate their own body heat, reptiles and amphibians are **ectothermic**—their body temperature and overall physiology rely on external conditions. In the wild, they thrive in carefully balanced ecosystems where temperature, humidity, vegetation, and shelter are in harmony.

When brought into captivity, their welfare depends on how closely these natural habitats can be replicated. A corn snake from the southeastern United States requires a warm, moderately humid environment with hiding places, while a dart frog from the Amazon rainforest needs constant high humidity, live vegetation, and access to water. Without understanding these natural environments, keepers risk creating enclosures that are aesthetically pleasing but biologically inadequate.

Thus, a detailed knowledge of natural habitats forms the backbone of responsible reptile and amphibian care.

3.2 Major Habitat Types and Their Features

1. Deserts and Arid Regions

- **Examples of inhabitants**: Bearded dragons (Pogona vitticeps), Uromastyx, horned lizards, desert tortoises.

- **Key features**: High daytime temperatures, cool nights, intense sunlight, low humidity, sandy or rocky terrain.

- **Implications in captivity**: Enclosures must include strong UVB lighting, a thermal gradient with basking spots, and dry substrates that mimic sandy or rocky soils. Humidity must be carefully controlled to prevent respiratory issues.

2. Tropical Rainforests

- **Examples of inhabitants**: Green tree pythons, dart frogs, chameleons, tokay geckos.

- **Key features**: Dense vegetation, high humidity (70–100%), frequent rainfall, moderate to warm temperatures, vertical space for climbing.

- **Implications in captivity**: Vivariums must include misting systems, live plants, climbing branches, and consistent humidity. Poor ventilation or lack of moisture leads to skin and respiratory problems.

3. Temperate Forests and Woodlands

- **Examples of inhabitants**: Corn snakes, box turtles, tiger salamanders.

- **Key features**: Seasonal variations in temperature, moderate humidity, leaf litter, and varied terrain.

- **Implications in captivity**: Enclosures must account for seasonal changes if breeding is intended, with leaf litter or forest-floor substrates. Hiding spots and moderate humidity levels are crucial.

4. Wetlands and Aquatic Environments

- **Examples of inhabitants**: Red-eared sliders, African dwarf frogs, axolotls, newts.

- **Key features**: Permanent or semi-permanent water bodies, aquatic vegetation, fluctuating water quality, basking sites for semi-aquatic species.

- **Implications in captivity**: Aquariums or semi-aquatic terrariums with filtration systems, safe water chemistry (pH, chlorine-free), and land/water divisions are essential.

5. Grasslands and Savannas

- **Examples of inhabitants**: Savanna monitors, sulcata tortoises, leopard tortoises.

- **Key features**: Open, sun-exposed areas with burrows, moderate rainfall, and seasonal variation.

- **Implications in captivity**: Large enclosures with deep substrate for digging, UVB exposure, and grazing vegetation. Many species from these habitats grow large and require outdoor pens in warm climates.

6. Montane (Mountainous) Regions

- **Examples of inhabitants**: Jackson's chameleons, mountain horned dragons, certain salamanders.

- **Key features**: Cooler temperatures, frequent mist, high elevation vegetation, and dramatic daily fluctuations.

- **Implications in captivity**: Lower temperatures must be provided compared to lowland tropical species, along with strong airflow, misting, and UV exposure.

By categorizing reptiles and amphibians by their native habitats, keepers gain insight into the environmental parameters needed for their survival and well-being.

3.3 Microhabitats: The Small-Scale Environment

While broad habitat categories are useful, reptiles and amphibians often thrive within **microhabitats**—specific niches within larger ecosystems. For example:

- A rainforest may host arboreal geckos living in tree canopies and terrestrial frogs dwelling among leaf litter.

- A desert may contain burrowing lizards that spend most of their lives underground, while others bask openly on rocks.

In captivity, enclosures should replicate not just the general biome but also the microhabitat. Arboreal animals need vertical climbing structures, while burrowers require deep, diggable substrates. Aquatic species may need shallow and deep zones within the same tank. Failure to consider microhabitats often results in stress, as animals cannot express their natural behaviors.

3.4 Climate and Environmental Cycles

Temperature   Cycles
In the wild, reptiles and amphibians experience natural fluctuations between day and night. Many also undergo seasonal changes that influence breeding behavior, metabolism, and activity levels. For example, temperate reptiles may brumate (a reptilian form of hibernation) during winter months.

In captivity, recreating these cycles—even on a smaller scale—is important. A basking area provides daytime heat, while cooler zones allow thermoregulation. For seasonal breeders, adjusting temperatures and photoperiods (light cycles) may trigger natural reproductive behaviors.

Humidity   and   Rainfall   Cycles
Amphibians, in particular, rely on seasonal rains for breeding.

Some frogs lay eggs only after heavy rainfall. In captivity, simulated rainstorms or increased misting can replicate these triggers.

Photoperiod   (Light   Cycles)
Day length influences hormonal cycles. Tropical species often require 12-hour light cycles year-round, while temperate species may need varied cycles to mimic seasonal changes. Using programmable timers ensures consistency.

Understanding and replicating these natural cycles enriches captive life and often leads to healthier, more active animals.

3.5 Substrates and Terrain Features

Natural habitats provide more than temperature and humidity—they offer **terrain and substrate** that animals use for burrowing, basking, climbing, or camouflage.

- **Desert species**: Sand, clay, and rocky surfaces. Captivity should use safe substrates (avoid loose sand for juveniles prone to impaction).

- **Forest species**: Leaf litter, soil, moss, bark. Bioactive substrates can replicate natural decomposition cycles.

- **Aquatic species**: Gravel, sand, or bare-bottom setups, depending on cleaning and safety.

- **Burrowing species**: Deep soil mixtures or coconut fiber substrates to allow digging.

Providing appropriate substrate enhances both physical and psychological health, allowing natural behaviors such as tunneling, hiding, or laying eggs.

3.6 The Role of Plants and Vegetation

In natural habitats, vegetation provides shade, moisture regulation, hiding spots, and food. In captivity, live plants are more than decorative—they are functional.

- **Humidity control**: Live plants increase humidity in rainforest setups.

- **Shelter**: Plants create hiding spots and reduce stress.

- **Diet**: Herbivorous reptiles and amphibians may graze on safe plants.

- **Aesthetics and enrichment**: Naturalistic enclosures mimic the wild environment, enriching the animal's experience and providing visual enjoyment for keepers.

Plant selection must prioritize safety, avoiding toxic species. Popular vivarium plants include pothos, bromeliads, ficus, and ferns for tropical enclosures.

3.7 Water Sources and Aquatic Features

For amphibians and many reptiles, water is central to habitat replication. In nature, water provides hydration, soaking areas, and breeding grounds.

- **Static water bowls**: Essential for hydration but must be cleaned daily.

- **Flowing water features**: Waterfalls and streams encourage natural behaviors but require filtration to prevent bacterial growth.

- **Aquatic habitats**: Full aquariums for axolotls, turtles, and aquatic frogs, requiring filtration and water-quality monitoring (pH, ammonia, nitrate levels).

Water quality is particularly critical for amphibians, whose permeable skin makes them highly susceptible to toxins. Always use dechlorinated or conditioned water in enclosures.

3.8 Habitat Complexity and Enrichment

A barren enclosure, even with correct temperatures and humidity, cannot substitute for a true habitat. Wild reptiles and amphibians engage in complex behaviors—climbing, hunting, hiding, and exploring. Captive environments must provide:

- **Climbing structures** (branches, vines, cork bark).

- **Hides** (caves, hollow logs, artificial hides).

- **Burrowing opportunities** (deep substrate, tunnels).

- **Basking platforms** (rocks, elevated spots).

Enclosure complexity reduces stress, encourages exercise, and allows natural behaviors, ultimately improving welfare.

3.9 Studying Habitat Before Ownership

Every responsible keeper should begin with research into the species' native environment:

- **Geographic range**: Where does the species occur naturally?

- **Climate data**: What are average temperatures, humidity, and rainfall?

- **Behavioral ecology**: Is the species nocturnal or diurnal? Arboreal or terrestrial? Solitary or social?

- **Seasonal changes**: Does the animal brumate, migrate, or breed seasonally?

Resources include scientific publications, field guides, reputable care sheets, and observations from experienced keepers. Without this foundation, captive care becomes guesswork—often at the animal's expense.

3.10 Conclusion: Building Nature Indoors

Understanding natural habitats is the cornerstone of reptile and amphibian care. These animals are not domesticated; their needs are written into their evolutionary history. By studying deserts, rainforests, wetlands, and beyond, keepers gain the knowledge required to replicate conditions that support both survival and thriving.

Captivity will never fully replicate the wild, but with careful attention to temperature, humidity, substrate, vegetation, and enrichment, keepers can create functional microcosms of nature. These enclosures not only safeguard animal health but also provide a window into the beauty and complexity of the natural world—a reminder that keeping reptiles and amphibians is both a responsibility and a privilege.

Chapter 4

Housing And Enclosure Design

4.1 The Importance of Proper Enclosures

For reptiles and amphibians, the enclosure is not just a cage—it is their entire world. Unlike cats or dogs, which roam homes and interact with their environment, reptiles and amphibians are fully dependent on the conditions inside their enclosures. Every element—temperature, lighting, substrate, humidity, shelter, and space—must be tailored to the species' natural needs.

An enclosure that is too small, barren, or poorly designed may cause chronic stress, suppress natural behaviors, weaken the immune system, and lead to premature death. Conversely, a well-planned enclosure supports physical health, mental well-being, and provides opportunities for natural activity such as climbing, digging, basking, or hunting.

Housing and enclosure design, therefore, is one of the most critical aspects of reptile and amphibian care.

4.2 Enclosure Types and Their Applications

1. Glass Terrariums

- **Advantages**: Excellent visibility, retain humidity well, suitable for tropical species, aesthetically pleasing.

- **Disadvantages**: Can trap heat, may be heavy, poor insulation in cold environments.

- **Best for**: Arboreal lizards, frogs, small snakes, and bioactive vivariums.

2. Wooden or PVC Enclosures

- **Advantages**: Excellent heat retention, customizable, durable, resistant to humidity (PVC).

- **Disadvantages**: Heavier, often less visually appealing, may require sealing against moisture.

- **Best for**: Large reptiles such as bearded dragons, tortoises, and snakes.

3. Aquariums and Semi-Aquatic Tanks

- **Advantages**: Necessary for aquatic and semi-aquatic species, allow water filtration and plant growth.

- **Disadvantages**: Can be difficult to maintain land-water balance, heavy, require regular water changes.

- **Best for**: Turtles, axolotls, newts, and aquatic frogs.

4. Mesh or Screen Cages

- **Advantages**: Excellent ventilation, prevent respiratory problems in certain species, lightweight.

- **Disadvantages**: Poor humidity retention, require frequent misting.

- **Best for**: Chameleons and arboreal lizards from well-ventilated environments.

5. Outdoor Enclosures

- **Advantages**: Provide natural sunlight, fresh air, space, and enrichment.

- **Disadvantages**: Dependent on climate, vulnerable to predators, require secure fencing.

- **Best for**: Large tortoises, iguanas, and some snakes in appropriate climates.

Selecting the right enclosure type depends on species, environmental needs, keeper's resources, and available space.

4.3 Enclosure Size Requirements

A golden rule of reptile and amphibian care is that **enclosures should prioritize the animal's adult size, not its juvenile size**. Many species start small but grow dramatically, often outgrowing beginner setups.

- **Snakes**: Minimum enclosure length should be at least two-thirds of the snake's full body length, with additional climbing space for arboreal species.

- **Lizards**: Enclosures should provide at least twice the length of the lizard in floor space, plus height for climbing species.

- **Tortoises**: Require large, horizontal enclosures with open floor space; many species thrive best in outdoor pens.

- **Amphibians**: Arboreal frogs need vertical space, while terrestrial species need more horizontal room with adequate substrate depth.

In all cases, **bigger is better**—provided environmental parameters can still be maintained.

4.4 Security and Escape Prevention

Reptiles and amphibians are adept escape artists. Snakes can slip through tiny gaps, lizards can climb and push lids, and turtles are surprisingly strong climbers. Secure housing prevents injury to the animal, household risks, and in some cases, environmental danger (escaped non-native species may become invasive).

- **Locks and Clips**: Always secure lids and doors.

- **Durable Materials**: Avoid flimsy plastic lids that can warp with heat.

- **Escape-Proof Ventilation**: Ensure mesh or vents are fine enough to prevent escapes but still allow airflow.

4.5 Environmental Control Systems

Heating

Reptiles require thermal gradients to regulate body temperature. Heating methods include:

- Heat lamps (basking bulbs).

- Ceramic heat emitters (infrared heat without light).

- Under-tank heating mats (for ground-dwelling species).

- Radiant heat panels (for large enclosures).

Lighting

- **UVB lighting** is essential for many reptiles to metabolize calcium and prevent metabolic bone disease.

- Amphibians typically require low to moderate light intensity, with UVB beneficial for some but not all species.

- Timers should be used to simulate natural day-night cycles.

Humidity

Maintaining correct humidity prevents dehydration, respiratory illness, and skin problems. Methods include:

- Manual misting.

- Automated misting or fogging systems.

- Humid hides (moist substrate in enclosed areas).

- Live plants to naturally regulate humidity.

Ventilation

Balance is key—tropical species require humidity without stagnant air, while arid species require airflow to prevent mold and bacterial buildup.

4.6 Substrate Choices

Substrates mimic the natural ground and influence humidity, burrowing, and egg-laying.

- **Desert species**: Clay-based sand blends or reptile-safe sand alternatives (avoid loose fine sand for juveniles).

- **Forest species**: Coconut fiber, soil, moss, and leaf litter for bioactive setups.

- **Aquatic setups**: Sand, gravel, or bare-bottom (for easy cleaning).

- **Burrowers**: Deep soil or soil-sand mixes for digging.

- **Paper towels/newspaper**: Practical for quarantine or medical treatment enclosures.

Toxic or unsafe substrates (e.g., cedar, pine shavings) must be avoided, as they release harmful oils.

4.7 Furnishings and Enclosure Enrichment

Hides   and   Shelters
 Every reptile or amphibian needs at least two hides: one in the warm zone and one in the cool zone. This allows thermoregulation while feeling secure.

Climbing   **Structures**

Branches, cork bark, vines, and shelves provide exercise and mimic natural arboreal environments.

Water   **Features**

From shallow bowls to complex streams and ponds, water sources must be clean and accessible. Amphibians often need soaking areas or fully aquatic setups.

Basking   **Platforms**

Rocks, logs, or artificial platforms positioned under heat lamps allow thermoregulation.

Live   **or**   **Artificial**   **Plants**

Provide cover, climbing surfaces, and humidity regulation.

Well-designed furnishings reduce stress, encourage exploration, and prevent stereotypic (abnormal repetitive) behaviors.

4.8 Bioactive Enclosures

Bioactive setups replicate miniature ecosystems with live plants, natural substrates, and decomposer organisms (springtails, isopods) to break down waste.

Advantages:

- Naturalistic, visually appealing.

- Self-sustaining waste management.

- Promotes natural behaviors.

Disadvantages:

- Higher initial setup cost.

- Requires ecological balance to avoid pest outbreaks.

- Not suitable for all species (large burrowers or destructive reptiles may disrupt systems).

Bioactive enclosures are especially effective for small lizards, frogs, and snakes in tropical habitats.

4.9 Hygiene and Maintenance

Even the best-designed enclosure requires consistent cleaning and monitoring:

- Spot clean daily (remove feces, uneaten food, shed skin).

- Disinfect water bowls and feeding areas regularly.

- Deep clean monthly, replacing substrates as needed.

- Monitor temperatures, humidity, and lighting with reliable tools.

Cleanliness prevents disease outbreaks, keeps odors under control, and ensures a safe environment for both the animal and keeper.

4.10 Designing with the Keeper in Mind

While enclosures must prioritize animal welfare, practicality for the keeper is equally important.

- **Accessibility**: Doors and lids should allow easy cleaning and feeding without stressing the animal.

- **Visibility**: Front-opening enclosures reduce stress compared to top-opening ones, where predators would normally strike from above.

- **Aesthetics**: A visually appealing terrarium can serve as a natural display in the home, fostering appreciation for the species.

- **Safety**: Heat sources should be shielded to prevent burns, and electrical systems must be secure from water exposure.

A balance between animal needs and keeper convenience ensures long-term success.

4.11 The Role of Outdoor Housing

Where climates allow, outdoor enclosures offer unparalleled benefits: natural sunlight, fresh air, seasonal variation, and large space.

- **Tortoises and turtles** often thrive in secure outdoor pens with access to natural grazing.

- **Large lizards and snakes** benefit from exposure to unfiltered UV rays.

However, outdoor housing requires predator-proof fencing, shade options, and strict climate monitoring. In unsuitable climates, indoor housing with artificial systems remains necessary.

4.12 Conclusion: Building a World Within Walls

Housing and enclosure design lies at the heart of reptile and amphibian care. More than a simple container, it is a living environment that must replicate the natural conditions of deserts, rainforests, wetlands, or savannas. Proper design empowers reptiles and amphibians to thermoregulate, explore, and thrive.

A well-constructed enclosure is also a work of art: a miniature ecosystem that educates, inspires, and enriches the lives of both animal and keeper. Success lies in combining scientific understanding with creativity and commitment, ensuring that every reptile or amphibian in captivity has a home that respects its natural history.

Chapter 5

Heating And Lighting

5.1 Why Heating and Lighting Are Critical

Reptiles and amphibians are **ectothermic** (cold-blooded), meaning they cannot regulate body temperature internally the way mammals and birds do. Instead, they depend on external sources—sunlight, warm surfaces, or shade—to achieve optimal body temperature. This is called **thermoregulation**, and it governs their ability to digest food, fight disease, reproduce, and remain active.

In captivity, enclosures must replicate these external energy sources through artificial heating and lighting systems. Without them, reptiles and amphibians cannot carry out normal physiological processes. For example:

- A snake kept too cold may refuse food or be unable to digest meals properly.

- A lizard without UVB lighting may suffer from metabolic bone disease.

- An amphibian exposed to excessive heat may dehydrate rapidly due to its permeable skin.

Heating and lighting, therefore, are not optional accessories—they are the very foundation of survival in captivity.

5.2 The Sun as a Model

In nature, the sun provides both **heat** (infrared radiation) and **light** (including visible and ultraviolet). Different species interact with sunlight in unique ways depending on their habitat.

- **Desert reptiles** bask openly in intense sun, absorbing both heat and UVB radiation.

- **Forest-dwelling amphibians** may live in shaded environments with diffuse light and stable humidity.

- **Aquatic turtles** bask on logs or rocks to absorb warmth and UVB between swimming sessions.

Replicating this balance in captivity requires careful selection of heat sources, UV lighting, and photoperiod control.

5.3 Heating Systems for Enclosures

1. Basking Bulbs (Incandescent or Halogen)

- Provide direct heat and visible light.

- Create basking spots similar to sunlight.

- Best for diurnal (day-active) reptiles like bearded dragons and iguanas.

- Should be positioned above a basking platform, with proper shielding to prevent burns.

2. Ceramic Heat Emitters (CHEs)

- Produce heat without light.

- Useful for maintaining nighttime warmth without disturbing natural day-night cycles.

- Long-lasting and efficient for larger enclosures.

3. Radiant Heat Panels

- Emit infrared heat over larger areas.

- Excellent for large snake or lizard enclosures where broad, even heating is required.

4. Under-Tank Heating Mats (UTHs)

- Provide belly heat by warming the substrate.

- Useful for ground-dwelling species like leopard geckos that absorb heat from below.

- Must be regulated with a thermostat to prevent burns or overheating.

5. Deep Heat Projectors (Infrared-A)

- Provide infrared heat similar to the sun's deep-penetrating warmth.

- Encourage natural basking behaviors and can be more efficient than older infrared methods.

6. Ambient Room Heating

- For very large enclosures or rooms housing multiple reptiles, space heaters can supplement enclosure-specific heating.

- Must always be paired with precise monitoring to avoid overheating.

5.4 The Concept of Thermal Gradients

In the wild, reptiles and amphibians move between sun and shade to regulate temperature. Captive enclosures must recreate this by providing **thermal gradients**:

- **Basking Zone**: A hot area directly under the heat source.

- **Cool Zone**: A shaded, cooler area away from the heat source.

- **Ambient Temperature**: The overall enclosure temperature between these zones.

This allows animals to self-regulate by choosing their preferred microclimate. A uniform enclosure temperature deprives them of this essential choice.

5.5 Temperature Monitoring and Control

Maintaining correct temperatures requires precise tools:

- **Thermometers**: Digital thermometers with probes provide accurate readings at basking and cool zones.

- **Infrared Thermometers (Temperature Guns)**: Allow quick surface readings of basking spots.

- **Thermostats**: Essential for regulating heaters and preventing dangerous overheating.

- **Hygrothermometers**: Combined tools that measure both humidity and temperature, useful for amphibians and rainforest reptiles.

Monitoring should occur daily, with adjustments made as needed based on seasonal changes or household conditions.

5.6 Lighting Requirements

1.   Visible   Light
All reptiles and amphibians benefit from a natural day-night rhythm. Brightness levels and spectrum should mimic natural conditions:

- **Desert species**: Require intense, bright lighting to simulate open sun.

- **Forest species**: Prefer more diffuse, shaded light.

- **Nocturnal species**: Need low light during the day and complete darkness at night.

2. **UVB** **Lighting**

Ultraviolet-B light is critical for many reptiles. It enables the synthesis of **vitamin D$_3$**, which allows the body to absorb and utilize calcium. Without UVB, reptiles are at risk of metabolic bone disease, characterized by weak, deformed bones and often fatal complications.

- **Desert species** (e.g., bearded dragons): Require high-output UVB (10–12%).

- **Forest species** (e.g., chameleons, geckos): Require moderate UVB (5–7%).

- **Nocturnal species** (e.g., leopard geckos, snakes): May obtain sufficient vitamin D$_3$ through dietary supplementation, though low UVB exposure can still be beneficial.

UVB lights must be replaced every 6–12 months, even if they appear to work, as their UV output diminishes over time.

3. **UVA** **Lighting**

Ultraviolet-A contributes to visible light spectrum perception. Many reptiles and amphibians can see UVA, and it influences natural behaviors such as feeding, mating, and activity cycles. Most high-quality UVB bulbs emit UVA as well.

4. **Full-Spectrum** **Lighting**

Specialized bulbs replicate both visible and UV spectrums,

creating naturalistic conditions that support both health and behavior.

5.7 Photoperiod and Light Cycles

Light cycles must mimic the animal's natural environment:

- **Tropical species**: Consistent 12-hour light cycles year-round.

- **Temperate species**: Variable cycles, longer days in summer and shorter days in winter.

- **Seasonal breeders**: Require changes in light cycles to trigger breeding behaviors.

Timers are invaluable for maintaining consistent day-night rhythms, reducing stress caused by irregular lighting schedules.

5.8 Special Considerations for Amphibians

Amphibians, with their permeable skin, have unique sensitivities:

- **Heat**: They are prone to overheating and dehydration. Gentle, indirect heating is preferable, often maintaining cooler enclosures than reptiles.

- **Light**: Many amphibians are nocturnal or crepuscular, avoiding bright light. UVB may be beneficial for some species, but lighting should remain subdued.

- **Humidity**: Amphibians rely more on humidity and water access than direct heat. Their setups often prioritize misting and water features over basking lamps.

Understanding these distinctions prevents common husbandry errors, such as overheating or exposing amphibians to overly bright light.

5.9 Common Mistakes in Heating and Lighting

1. **Using Inadequate Bulbs**
   Desk lamps or household bulbs cannot substitute for reptile-specific heat or UVB lamps.

2. **Ignoring Nighttime Needs**
   Providing bright light at night disrupts circadian rhythms. Heat-only emitters or ceramic heaters should be used for nighttime warmth.

3. **Placing Bulbs Too Far**
   UVB effectiveness decreases with distance. Lamps must be installed at the correct height, usually 8–18 inches from the basking surface depending on the bulb type.

4. **Overheating Enclosures**
   Too much heat with no cool zone prevents thermoregulation and can cause fatal heat stress.

5. **Neglecting Replacement Schedules**
   UVB bulbs lose effectiveness after 6–12 months. Failing to replace them on time results in invisible but dangerous deficiencies.

5.10 Energy Efficiency and Safety

Heating and lighting systems often run for long hours, increasing energy costs. Keepers can reduce waste while maintaining animal welfare by:

- Using thermostats and timers to control usage.

- Selecting energy-efficient bulbs (e.g., T5 HO UVB tubes instead of compact fluorescents).

- Insulating enclosures to retain heat.

Safety is equally important:

- All heating devices must be shielded to prevent burns.

- Electrical systems should be protected from water in amphibian setups.

- Power strips with surge protection reduce fire risks.

5.11 Integrating Heating and Lighting into Enclosure Design

Heating and lighting cannot be considered in isolation—they must integrate with the entire enclosure design:

- Basking lamps should be positioned over rocks or branches to create realistic basking spots.

- UVB tubes should run across the enclosure's length to provide broad coverage.

- Hides should exist in both warm and cool zones, allowing secure thermoregulation.

- Water sources should be placed away from heating elements to prevent rapid evaporation and mold.

An enclosure designed with heating and lighting in mind promotes both functionality and aesthetics.

5.12 Conclusion: Replicating the Sun Indoors

Heating and lighting are the lifeblood of reptile and amphibian care. They replicate the sun—the ultimate source of warmth and energy in the natural world. By carefully selecting and arranging heating devices, UVB systems, and photoperiod schedules, keepers create environments that allow their animals to thrive, not merely survive.

Mistakes in this area are among the most common causes of illness and death in captivity, but with knowledge and attention, they are also the most preventable. Success lies in precision, consistency, and respect for the animal's natural needs.

A well-lit, properly heated enclosure is more than a technical setup—it is an investment in the health, longevity, and natural behavior of some of Earth's most remarkable creatures.

Chapter 6

Temperature And Humidity Control

6.1 Why Temperature and Humidity Matter

Reptiles and amphibians live within carefully balanced ecosystems where temperature and humidity dictate survival. Because they are **ectothermic**, reptiles depend on environmental warmth to regulate metabolism, digestion, reproduction, and immune function. Amphibians, with their thin, permeable skin, are especially sensitive to moisture levels, relying on humidity and water availability to avoid dehydration and support respiration.

In captivity, failing to maintain correct temperature and humidity is one of the most common—and dangerous—mistakes keepers make. Animals may survive for a time, but without proper regulation they experience stress, illness, and ultimately premature death.

Mastering temperature and humidity control is therefore not simply about comfort—it is about replicating nature closely enough to support life and natural behavior.

6.2 The Role of Thermal and Moisture Gradients

In the wild, animals do not live in uniform climates. Even within the same habitat, microclimates exist: shaded burrows, sunny rocks, damp leaf litter, or misty canopy layers. Animals move between these zones to maintain equilibrium.

Captive enclosures must recreate these options through **gradients**:

- **Thermal Gradient**: A range of temperatures from a hot basking zone to a cooler resting zone. This allows reptiles to self-regulate.

- **Moisture Gradient**: Areas of higher and lower humidity within the same enclosure, enabling amphibians and reptiles to choose what suits them best at a given time.

Providing gradients respects natural behavior and prevents health issues caused by being locked into unsuitable conditions.

6.3 Temperature Control in Captivity

1.   Basking   Zones   and   Ambient   Heat
Every reptile enclosure should include:

- **Basking area**: Direct heat source where the animal can raise its body temperature.

- **Ambient zone**: The middle ground of the enclosure, providing stable background warmth.

- **Cool zone**: A shaded or distant area for cooling down.

2. Species-Specific Temperature Ranges

- **Desert reptiles (e.g., bearded dragons, uromastyx)**: Basking spots 38–45°C (100–113°F), cool zones 24–29°C (75–85°F).

- **Temperate reptiles (e.g., corn snakes, box turtles)**: Basking spots 29–32°C (85–90°F), cool zones 21–24°C (70–75°F).

- **Rainforest reptiles (e.g., green tree pythons, chameleons)**: Moderate basking 30–32°C (86–90°F), cooler ambient 24–27°C (75–80°F).

- **Amphibians (e.g., dart frogs, salamanders)**: Lower temperatures, usually 18–25°C (65–77°F), depending on species.

3. Seasonal Adjustments

Some reptiles, especially temperate-zone species, rely on

seasonal changes. Brumation (a reptilian form of hibernation) may be necessary for health or breeding. Controlled cooling periods, with reduced heat and light cycles, should be researched for species-specific needs.

6.4 Tools for Measuring and Regulating Temperature

- **Digital Thermometers with Probes**: Offer accurate readings at basking and cool zones.

- **Infrared Temperature Guns**: Allow surface checks of rocks, branches, and basking spots.

- **Thermostats**: Essential for regulating heaters, preventing overheating and maintaining consistency.

- **Temperature Controllers with Dimmers**: Provide fine adjustments, especially for sensitive amphibians.

Consistency in monitoring is as important as the equipment itself. Enclosures should be checked daily, as household conditions and weather can alter temperatures unexpectedly.

6.5 Humidity: The Other Half of the Equation

1.   Importance   of   Humidity
Humidity affects hydration, skin health, shedding, and respiratory function. Amphibians, in particular, require moist environments for cutaneous respiration and egg development. Many reptiles, though less moisture-dependent, still rely on humidity for proper shedding and hydration.

2. Species-Specific Humidity Ranges

- **Desert species (e.g., leopard geckos, uromastyx)**: 20–40%.

- **Tropical forest species (e.g., dart frogs, chameleons)**: 70–100%.

- **Temperate species (e.g., corn snakes, salamanders)**: 50–70%.

- **Aquatic and semi-aquatic species (e.g., turtles, newts)**: Water access is more critical, but ambient humidity 60–80% supports skin and shell health.

3. Dangers of Incorrect Humidity

- **Too low**: Dehydration, incomplete shedding, respiratory issues.

- **Too high**: Mold, bacterial overgrowth, skin infections, respiratory illness.

Balance is crucial—humidity should match the natural environment, not exceed it.

6.6 Methods of Regulating Humidity

1. Misting

- Manual spraying with a fine mist bottle.

- Automated misting systems for rainforest species requiring frequent hydration.

2. Fogging Machines

- Produce cool mist, ideal for tropical setups.

- Best used in combination with ventilation to prevent stagnation.

3. Water Dishes and Pools

- Increase localized humidity through evaporation.

- Amphibians and many reptiles drink directly from shallow dishes.

4. Substrate Choice

- Moisture-retentive substrates (e.g., coconut fiber, sphagnum moss) increase humidity.

- Arid substrates (e.g., sand, clay blends) prevent excessive humidity.

5. Live Plants

- Naturally increase humidity through transpiration.

- Also provide shelter and aesthetic enrichment.

6.7 Tools for Measuring Humidity

- **Hygrometers**: Digital probes are more reliable than analogue dial versions.

- **Data Loggers**: Advanced devices that record fluctuations over time, useful for sensitive amphibians.

- **Combination Meters**: Devices that track both temperature and humidity simultaneously.

Placement of sensors matters—measure at both substrate level and mid-air, as readings can vary widely within a single enclosure.

6.8 Microclimates Within Enclosures

Creating varied conditions within a single enclosure allows animals to choose where to spend time:

- **Humid hides**: Enclosed spaces filled with moist moss or substrate help snakes and lizards shed properly.

- **Basking ledges**: Warm, dry zones under lamps mimic sunlit rocks.

- **Cool retreats**: Burrows or shaded areas for rest.

- **Aquatic/terrestrial divisions**: Semi-aquatic enclosures provide both dry basking zones and humid aquatic areas.

These microclimates reduce stress and promote natural behaviors, such as alternating between sunning, burrowing, or soaking.

6.9 Ventilation and Airflow

While humidity is essential, stagnant air fosters mold and bacterial growth. Proper ventilation is as important as misting systems.

- **Screen lids** provide airflow but may reduce humidity—best for species needing high ventilation (chameleons).

- **Partially covered enclosures** balance airflow with moisture retention.

- **Fans or air circulation systems** (gentle, not drying) can be used for large enclosures.

The goal is to balance moisture with freshness—mimicking natural breezes, not sealed dampness.

6.10 Common Mistakes in Temperature and Humidity Control

1. **Relying on Room Temperature**
   Household conditions are rarely suitable for reptiles or amphibians without supplemental heating or humidity.

2. **Uniform Temperatures**
   Providing the same heat level throughout the enclosure prevents natural thermoregulation.

3. **Over-Misting**
   Leads to excessively wet enclosures, mold, and respiratory infections.

4. **Ignoring Nighttime Drops**
   Many species require cooler nights to replicate natural cycles. Constant high heat can stress animals.

5. **Using Inaccurate Gauges**
   Cheap thermometers and hygrometers often give misleading readings, leading to incorrect adjustments.

6.11 Advanced Systems for Climate Control

1.   **Thermostatically   Controlled   Heating**
Ensures heat sources shut off when optimal temperatures are reached, preventing overheating.

2.   Automated   Misting   and   Fogging
Provide consistent humidity for rainforest setups without constant manual effort.

3.   Climate   Controllers
Integrate heating, lighting, humidity, and ventilation into one automated   system.
These are ideal for keepers maintaining multiple enclosures or sensitive species.

6.12 Special Considerations for Amphibians

Because of their delicate physiology, amphibians have unique challenges:

- **Permeable skin**: Even small deviations in humidity can cause dehydration or stress.

- **Cool preferences**: Amphibians often thrive in cooler environments, unlike reptiles that seek higher basking temperatures.

- **Water quality**: Amphibians absorb water through their skin, making clean, dechlorinated water vital.

- **Breeding cycles**: Many amphibians respond to simulated rainy seasons, requiring precise manipulation of temperature and humidity.

Amphibian setups demand extra diligence in monitoring both temperature and moisture stability.

6.13 Case Study Examples

- **Bearded Dragon**: Requires basking zones of 40°C (104°F) with low humidity (~30%). Overly moist conditions cause respiratory distress.

- **Dart Frog**: Thrives at 24°C (75°F) with 80–100% humidity. Inadequate humidity results in desiccation and early death.

- **Corn Snake**: Prefers a gradient from 21–29°C (70–85°F) with 50–60% humidity. Humid hides assist during shedding.

- **Red-Eared Slider**: Requires aquatic water temperatures of 24–27°C (75–80°F) and basking platforms reaching 32°C (90°F).

Each example illustrates how different species demand unique microclimates, reinforcing the need for research before setup.

6.14 Conclusion: Creating Balance in Captivity

Temperature and humidity control lies at the heart of reptile and amphibian care. These parameters are not luxuries but biological necessities, influencing every aspect of health, from digestion to skin shedding, hydration, and breeding.

By replicating thermal and moisture gradients, keepers offer animals the ability to self-regulate, just as they do in the wild. This requires attention to detail, reliable equipment, and daily monitoring—but the reward is vibrant, active animals displaying natural behaviors.

The most successful keepers are those who view enclosures not as static cages but as dynamic microclimates, adjusted and maintained with respect for the animal's evolutionary history. Achieving this balance is both a science and an art—and it is the keeper's duty to master it.

Chapter 7

Diet And Nutrition

7.1 Introduction: Why Diet Matters

Reptiles and amphibians have evolved highly specialized feeding strategies suited to their ecological niches. From insect-hunting geckos to grazing tortoises, piscivorous (fish-eating) turtles, and ambush-predator snakes, each species' nutritional needs are unique.

Unlike mammals, which often tolerate a broad diet range, reptiles and amphibians are less adaptable. A poor diet leads quickly to **nutritional deficiencies, metabolic disorders, obesity, organ failure, and shortened lifespans**. Conversely, a diet that closely mirrors natural feeding patterns ensures vibrant coloration, strong skeletal development, healthy immune systems, and natural activity.

Understanding diet and nutrition is therefore central to responsible herpetological husbandry.

7.2 Categories of Diet Types

1. Insectivores

- Rely primarily on insects and other invertebrates.

- Examples: Leopard geckos, chameleons, dart frogs.

- Common feeders: Crickets, roaches, mealworms, silkworms, black soldier fly larvae.

2. Carnivores

- Eat vertebrate prey such as rodents, birds, or fish.

- Examples: Snakes, monitor lizards, some aquatic turtles.

- Feeding method: Usually whole-prey feeding to provide complete nutrition.

3. Herbivores

- Consume plant-based diets—leaves, grasses, flowers, fruits.

- Examples: Iguanas, tortoises, uromastyx.

- Require high fiber, low protein, and calcium-rich greens.

4. Omnivores

- Eat a mixture of plant and animal matter.

- Examples: Bearded dragons, box turtles, some frogs.

- Diet balance shifts with age; many are more insectivorous as juveniles and more herbivorous as adults.

5. Specialized Diets

- Some species have highly specific needs:

  - **Snail-eating snakes** rely on mollusks.

  - **Filter-feeding tadpoles** consume algae and detritus.

  - **Frogs such as horned frogs** consume large prey including small vertebrates.

7.3 Principles of Nutrition

1. Macronutrients

- **Proteins**: Essential for growth, repair, and reproduction. Insectivores and carnivores rely heavily on protein-rich diets.

- **Fats**: Provide energy but must be balanced; excessive fat leads to obesity and fatty liver disease.

- **Carbohydrates**: Play a minor role; herbivores benefit from fiber-rich vegetation rather than starchy foods.

2. Micronutrients

- **Calcium**: Critical for bone development and muscle function. A deficiency leads to metabolic bone disease (MBD).

- **Phosphorus**: Must be balanced with calcium. Ideal Ca:P ratio is about **2:1**.

- **Vitamins**:

  - **Vitamin D$_3$**: Works with calcium; synthesized via UVB exposure or supplemented in diet.

- ○ **Vitamin A**: Important for vision and skin; deficiency causes "short tongue syndrome" in lizards and poor eye health in amphibians.

- ○ **Vitamin E and K**: Needed in trace amounts for cellular health and blood clotting.

- **Minerals**: Magnesium, potassium, iron, and iodine support general metabolism.

7.4 Feeding Insectivores

Staple Insects

- Crickets: Widely available but low in calcium.

- Dubia roaches: Nutritious, long-lived, and less likely to escape than crickets.

- Black soldier fly larvae: Naturally high in calcium.

- Silkworms: Soft-bodied and protein-rich.

Occasional Insects

- Mealworms and superworms: High in fat and chitin; fed sparingly.

- Waxworms: Extremely fatty; treat only.

- Wild-caught insects: Risk of pesticide contamination—best avoided unless verified safe.

Gut-Loading and Dusting

- **Gut-loading**: Feeding insects a nutritious diet (greens, grains, supplements) 24–48 hours before offering them. This passes nutrients to the reptile or amphibian.

- **Dusting**: Coating feeders with calcium and vitamin powders to prevent deficiencies.

Feeding Frequency

- Juveniles: Daily feeding to support rapid growth.

- Adults: Every other day or 2–3 times per week, depending on species.

7.5 Feeding Carnivores

Whole   Prey   Principle
Feeding whole prey (e.g., mice, rats, fish) ensures balanced nutrition, including bones, organs, and muscle. Meat-only diets (like chicken breast) are dangerously incomplete.

Prey Size

- Should be no larger than the widest part of the reptile's body.

- Overly large prey risks regurgitation or internal damage.

Frozen-Thawed vs. Live Prey

- **Frozen-thawed** (properly thawed and warmed) is recommended—safer, more humane, and nutritionally equivalent.

- **Live prey** poses risks of injury to the predator and is considered inhumane unless absolutely necessary.

Feeding Frequency

- Juvenile snakes: Every 5–7 days.

- Adult snakes: Every 10–21 days depending on size.

- Large monitors and crocodilians: Weekly or biweekly.

7.6 Feeding Herbivores

Staple Foods

- Dark leafy greens: Collard, mustard, dandelion, turnip greens.

- Edible flowers: Hibiscus, nasturtium, hibiscus, squash blossoms.

- Grasses and weeds: Bermuda grass, clover, plantain.

Foods to Limit

- Fruits: High sugar content, fed sparingly.

- Kale and spinach: Contain oxalates that bind calcium, should be limited.

Supplements

- Calcium powder: Essential for bone strength.

- Vitamin D_3: Necessary if UVB exposure is inadequate.

Feeding Frequency

- Herbivores typically require daily feeding with constant access to fresh greens.

7.7 Feeding Omnivores

Omnivores require a careful balance of both plant and animal matter.

- **Juvenile bearded dragons**: ~70% insects, 30% plants.

- **Adult bearded dragons**: ~70% plants, 30% insects.

- **Box turtles**: Mix of worms, insects, mushrooms, and greens.

Balance must adjust with age and natural biology. Overfeeding protein to omnivores predisposed to herbivory (like adult dragons) leads to kidney and liver problems.

7.8 Amphibian Diets

Frogs and Toads

- Primarily insectivorous.

- Larger species (e.g., horned frogs, bullfrogs) may eat small vertebrates.

Salamanders and Newts

- Worms, insects, small crustaceans, and occasionally small fish.

Aquatic Amphibians (e.g., Axolotls)

- Worms, pellets, small fish.

- Require sinking food items, as they often feed near the bottom.

Tadpoles

- Many are herbivorous filter-feeders consuming algae and biofilm.

- Some are omnivorous or carnivorous depending on species.

7.9 Supplements and Nutritional Aids

- **Calcium powder**: Essential for most reptiles, especially fast-growing juveniles and egg-laying females.

- **Vitamin D$_3$ supplements**: Needed if UVB exposure is inadequate.

- **Multivitamin powders**: Should be used sparingly; oversupplementation can be as harmful as deficiencies.

- **Specialized diets**: Commercial pellets exist for turtles, axolotls, and some lizards. While convenient, they should be supplemented with fresh foods for variety.

7.10 Hydration and Feeding

Hydration is directly tied to diet.

- Many amphibians absorb water from moist food or the environment.

- Reptiles like chameleons often refuse standing water, instead drinking droplets from misted leaves.

- Herbivores gain much of their hydration from leafy greens.

A feeding routine must consider hydration needs alongside caloric intake.

7.11 Feeding Techniques and Safety

- **Tongs or Feeding Tweezers**: Prevent accidental bites when feeding carnivores or aggressive feeders.

- **Separate Feeding Enclosures**: Reduce substrate ingestion and aggressive competition in communal setups.

- **Observation**: Monitoring feeding ensures that shy or submissive animals are not outcompeted.

7.12 Common Feeding Mistakes

1. **Monotonous Diets**
   Feeding the same insect or green repeatedly leads to deficiencies. Variety is essential.

2. **Overfeeding**
   Causes obesity, fatty liver disease, and shortened lifespans.

3. **Under-Supplementing Calcium**
   One of the most common causes of metabolic bone disease.

4. **Offering Unsafe Foods**
   Examples: Iceberg lettuce (nutritionally empty), avocados (toxic), citrus (too acidic).

5. **Improper Prey Size**
   Feeding prey that is too large risks regurgitation and injury.

7.13 The Role of Observation in Nutrition

Each reptile or amphibian is an individual. Careful observation helps detect problems early:

- **Weight monitoring** ensures animals are neither underfed nor obese.

- **Shedding quality** reflects hydration and mineral balance.

- **Appetite changes** may signal illness or improper environmental conditions.

Feeding is not just about providing calories—it is about ensuring optimal long-term health.

7.14 Conclusion: Feeding for Longevity and Health

Diet and nutrition form the cornerstone of reptile and amphibian care. Providing the right balance of proteins, fats, vitamins, and minerals is as important as replicating natural habitats. The goal is not simply to keep animals alive but to allow them to **thrive**—to grow, reproduce, and display their natural behaviors.

By studying species-specific needs, providing varied and balanced diets, supplementing wisely, and avoiding common pitfalls, keepers ensure that their reptiles and amphibians live long, healthy, and fulfilling lives. Feeding, in this sense, becomes more than husbandry—it becomes stewardship.

Chapter 8

Hydration and Water Features

8.1 Introduction: The Central Role of Water

Water is the foundation of all life, and for reptiles and amphibians it is especially critical. Unlike mammals and birds, which have efficient internal water conservation mechanisms, many reptiles and nearly all amphibians are highly dependent on their external environment for hydration.

- **Reptiles** regulate hydration through drinking, food moisture, and environmental humidity.

- **Amphibians** absorb water directly through their permeable skin and require access to moist environments to survive.

In captivity, improper hydration is one of the leading causes of health problems, ranging from kidney failure to skin infections and incomplete shedding. Designing appropriate **hydration systems and water features** is therefore not an accessory, but an essential component of reptile and amphibian husbandry.

8.2 Methods of Hydration in Reptiles and Amphibians

1. Drinking from Standing Water

- Many reptiles (e.g., snakes, tortoises, aquatic turtles) drink directly from bowls or pools.

- Amphibians rarely rely on standing water, though aquatic species may swallow water incidentally while feeding.

2. Drinking from Moving Water

- Some reptiles, such as chameleons and anoles, rarely recognize standing water. They instinctively drink from droplets on leaves or from trickling water.

- In captivity, misting systems or drippers simulate this natural behavior.

3. Absorption through Skin (Amphibians)

- Amphibians rely heavily on cutaneous absorption through specialized regions called "drink patches" (usually on the belly and thighs).

- This means hydration is less about drinking and more about environmental humidity and moist surfaces.

4. Food-Derived Moisture

- Herbivorous reptiles obtain much of their hydration from water-rich greens and fruits.

- Insectivores gain hydration indirectly from their prey, especially if feeders are well-hydrated before offering.

8.3 Designing Water Features for Captive Care

1. Water Bowls

- Should be shallow enough to prevent drowning in small species, but large enough for soaking in others.

- Smooth, easy-to-clean surfaces (ceramic, stainless steel, heavy-duty plastic) are best.

- Must be placed away from heat lamps to prevent rapid evaporation and bacterial growth.

2. Ponds and Pools

- Essential for aquatic or semi-aquatic species such as sliders, newts, and salamanders.

- Require filtration to maintain water quality.

- Depth and access must match the species: turtles need basking platforms, while amphibians require easy exits.

3. Drippers and Rain Systems

- Mimic natural rainfall or dripping water for arboreal species like chameleons.

- Provide hydration and increase enclosure humidity.

- Must be monitored to avoid excess water pooling and mold growth.

4. Fogging and Misting Systems

- Create fine droplets in the air, simulating rainforest or cloud forest conditions.

- Amphibians and tropical reptiles often drink from or absorb this mist.

- Automated systems offer consistency, reducing keeper workload.

8.4 Water Quality and Safety

1. Dechlorination

- Tap water often contains chlorine or chloramines, which are harmful to amphibians and some reptiles.

- Dechlorination drops or water conditioners should always be used, or water left to sit for 24–48 hours to off-gas chlorine (not effective for chloramine).

2. Filtration Systems

- Aquatic enclosures require filtration to prevent ammonia and waste buildup.

- Types include:

  - Sponge filters (gentle, ideal for amphibians and fry).

  - Canister filters (powerful, suitable for turtle tanks).

  - Internal power filters (compact, easy to maintain).

3. Temperature Control in Water

- Water temperature must match species needs.

- Cold water stresses tropical amphibians, while overly warm water reduces oxygen levels.

- Heaters with thermostats ensure consistency.

4. Hygiene

- Water dishes must be cleaned and disinfected daily, as reptiles often defecate in their bowls.

- Aquatic setups require regular partial water changes, even with filtration.

8.5 Hydration Needs by Habitat Type

1. Desert Reptiles

- Appear adapted to dryness but still require hydration opportunities.

- Shallow bowls or occasional misting for species like leopard geckos.

- Herbivores (e.g., uromastyx) obtain much water from fresh greens.

2. Tropical Forest Species

- High humidity and frequent misting required.

- Arboreal lizards (chameleons, anoles) need dripping or sprayed water on leaves.

- Amphibians thrive with constant access to moist hides and misted enclosures.

3. Aquatic and Semi-Aquatic Species

- Must have access to swimming areas.

- Require basking zones to prevent constant wetness, which can cause shell or skin issues.

4. Temperate Species

- Need seasonal variation in water availability.

- Box turtles, for example, require soaking areas but may spend time in drier spots during brumation periods.

8.6 Amphibian-Specific Water Concerns

Amphibians are uniquely tied to water quality because of their permeable skin.

- **Absorption Risks**: Amphibians can absorb toxins, heavy metals, or pesticides directly through skin. Even mild contaminants are dangerous.

- **Oxygenation**: Stagnant water can suffocate amphibians, especially larvae. Aeration or plants improve oxygen levels.

- **Breeding Cues**: Many amphibians require water features for reproduction. Seasonal "rain" simulations encourage calling, mating, and egg-laying.

- **Larval Care**: Tadpoles often require algae-rich water or specialized foods, with careful monitoring of ammonia and pH.

8.7 Dehydration and Overhydration

Signs of Dehydration

- Sunken eyes.

- Wrinkled or sagging skin.

- Lethargy, weakness.

- Dry, incomplete shedding.

Causes

- Inadequate humidity.

- Lack of clean water sources.

- Overheating from poor temperature regulation.

Signs of Overhydration (Waterlogging)

- Swollen body.

- Loss of balance or bloating.

- Skin damage in amphibians exposed to constantly saturated conditions.

Prevention

- Balance hydration with ventilation.

- Provide water in moderation for species adapted to drier habitats.

8.8 The Role of Plants in Hydration Systems

- **Live Plants** increase ambient humidity through transpiration.

- **Leaf Surfaces** provide natural drinking platforms for arboreal reptiles.

- **Aquatic Plants** help filter water, oxygenate aquatic setups, and provide shelter for amphibians.

- Must be safe and non-toxic; some common houseplants are dangerous if ingested.

8.9 Enclosure Design for Water Management

- **Drainage Layers**: Essential in bioactive enclosures to prevent waterlogging.

- **Waterproof Barriers**: Prevent leaks and maintain humidity levels.

- **Placement of Water Bowls**: Avoid under basking lamps to reduce bacterial growth.

- **Accessibility**: Ensure animals can easily enter and exit water features without risk of drowning.

8.10 Common Mistakes in Hydration and Water Features

1. **Using Distilled Water Exclusively**
   Devoid of minerals, it may cause osmotic stress in amphibians and reptiles. Mineral-balanced or conditioned tap water is preferable.

2. **Neglecting Hygiene**
   Dirty water bowls are breeding grounds for bacteria and parasites.

3. **Over-Misting**
   Leads to stagnant, overly wet environments that

foster mold.

4. **Improper Depth**
   Deep water dishes can drown hatchlings or small amphibians.

5. **Ignoring Species-Specific Needs**
   A chameleon will ignore standing water, while a tortoise may not drink without soaking opportunities.

8.11 Case Study Examples

- **Chameleons**: Require drippers or misting; often die of dehydration in captivity if provided only bowls.

- **Dart Frogs**: Thrive with daily misting and bromeliads that collect water droplets.

- **Red-Eared Sliders**: Need full aquatic setups with filtration and a basking dock.

- **Leopard Geckos**: Live in arid regions but need a moist hide to aid shedding.

These examples highlight the diverse strategies reptiles and amphibians use to maintain hydration.

8.12 Conclusion: Water as the Lifeblood of Husbandry

Hydration and water features are not decorative elements—they are vital lifelines for reptiles and amphibians. The success of an enclosure depends on the keeper's ability to replicate natural hydration methods: rain, dew, streams, ponds, or water-rich vegetation.

Whether through carefully maintained water bowls, complex aquatic systems, misting routines, or bioactive ecosystems, keepers must ensure their animals have safe, consistent access to hydration.

Ultimately, water management is about balance: enough to sustain life and health without fostering harmful conditions. By respecting this delicate balance, we safeguard the well-being of these remarkable creatures and bring captivity closer to the thriving conditions of the wild.

Chapter 9

Substrates And Furnishings

9.1 Introduction: The Importance of Ground and Structure

When people think of reptile or amphibian care, they often focus on heating, lighting, and diet. Yet the **substrate** (the material covering the enclosure floor) and **furnishings** (the structural features inside the habitat) are equally crucial. These elements determine not only the look of the enclosure but also the health, comfort, and behavior of its inhabitants.

A poorly chosen substrate may cause impaction, harbor harmful bacteria, or fail to retain proper humidity. Inadequate furnishings may leave animals stressed, exposed, or unable to express natural behaviors such as burrowing, climbing, basking, or hiding. On the other hand, thoughtfully selected substrates and furnishings transform an enclosure into a functional microhabitat that mirrors nature.

9.2 The Role of Substrates in Husbandry

Substrates serve multiple functions:

- **Environmental Regulation**: Influence temperature and humidity retention.

- **Behavioral Expression**: Allow digging, burrowing, nesting, or moisture absorption.

- **Hygiene and Health**: Affect cleanliness and parasite control.

- **Aesthetics**: Provide naturalistic appearance, making enclosures more appealing.

Because reptiles and amphibians vary widely in habitat—from deserts to rainforests to aquatic environments—substrate choice must always be **species-specific**.

9.3 Types of Substrates

1. Desert and Arid Substrates

- **Sand blends**: Provide a natural look but pose impaction risks if ingested in excess. Safer when mixed with clay or soil to form a packed, diggable surface.

- **Excavator clay**: Allows reptiles to dig stable burrows.

- **Paper towels or reptile carpet**: Low-maintenance alternatives for young or small desert reptiles, though they lack natural aesthetics.

2. Tropical and Humid Substrates

- **Coconut fiber (coir)**: Excellent moisture retention, mold-resistant, safe for burrowing.

- **Sphagnum moss**: Retains moisture for humid hides; not suitable as the sole substrate.

- **Soil mixes**: Organic topsoil (pesticide-free) blended with sand and moss, creating bioactive bases for rainforest setups.

- **Leaf litter**: Mimics forest floors, enriches microclimates, and supports bioactive enclosures.

3. Semi-Aquatic and Aquatic Substrates

- **River pebbles**: Smooth, prevent ingestion in turtles.

- **Aquatic sand**: Creates natural underwater flooring but requires regular cleaning.

- **Bare-bottom tanks**: Simplify cleaning and are often used in amphibian aquaria, though less naturalistic.

4. Temporary or Quarantine Substrates

- **Paper towels, butcher paper, or newspaper**: Easy to clean and replace, ideal for monitoring health in new or sick animals.

9.4 Substrate Hazards

- **Impaction**: Ingestion of loose substrates (sand, gravel) can block the digestive tract, especially in juveniles.

- **Toxicity**: Fertilized soils or treated woods may poison reptiles and amphibians.

- **Moisture Mismatch**: Using overly dry substrates for humidity-dependent species (or vice versa) causes dehydration or respiratory problems.

- **Mold and Bacteria**: Overly wet, stagnant substrates encourage harmful microbial growth.

Keepers must research the **natural substrate of the species** and replicate it safely.

9.5 The Role of Furnishings

Furnishings provide structure and enrichment inside enclosures. They:

- Offer hiding places to reduce stress.

- Provide climbing and basking opportunities.

- Create microclimates (e.g., humid hides).

- Stimulate natural foraging and exploration behaviors.

Without adequate furnishings, reptiles and amphibians may become lethargic, stressed, or aggressive.

9.6 Essential Furnishings

1. Hides

- Every enclosure should have at least **two hides**: one in the warm zone and one in the cool zone.

- **Humid hides** filled with damp moss or substrate aid shedding.

- Secure hides reduce stress by offering safe retreats.

2. Climbing Structures

- Branches, cork bark, and vines for arboreal reptiles like chameleons or tree frogs.

- Must be stable and positioned under lighting for basking species.

3. Basking Platforms

- Rocks, logs, or shelves placed under heat lamps.

- Flat, stable surfaces prevent accidents.

4. Water Features

- Pools, dishes, or integrated ponds, depending on species.

- Must be easy to clean to prevent contamination.

5. Substrate-Integrated Furnishings

- Burrows, tunnels, and dig boxes encourage natural digging behavior in snakes, skinks, and tortoises.

9.7 Naturalistic and Bioactive Furnishings

Bioactive enclosures replicate natural ecosystems by incorporating living plants, microfauna (e.g., springtails, isopods), and natural materials. Benefits include:

- Self-cleaning capabilities through detritivore activity.

- Stable humidity and microclimates.

- More natural and enriching habitats for the animal.

Common materials include:

- Cork bark (lightweight, rot-resistant).

- Driftwood (provides climbing and aesthetic appeal).

- Rocks (offer basking platforms, but must be secured to prevent collapse).

- Live plants (safe, non-toxic species that also aid humidity).

9.8 Amphibian-Specific Furnishing Needs

Amphibians require particular care due to their permeable skin:

- **Moist shelters**: Hides filled with moss or leaf litter to maintain hydration.

- **Aquatic areas**: Smooth stones or floating plants for resting.

- **Gentle surfaces**: Avoid sharp rocks or rough wood that could damage delicate skin.

- **Cover**: Dense foliage or structures to reduce stress from exposure.

Because amphibians are sensitive to toxins, all furnishing materials must be untreated and thoroughly cleaned.

9.9 Hygiene and Maintenance

Both substrates and furnishings can harbor waste, bacteria, and parasites if neglected. Best practices include:

- **Spot cleaning**: Remove feces and uneaten food daily.

- **Deep cleaning**: Replace or sanitize substrates and furnishings regularly (frequency depends on enclosure type).

- **Bioactive systems**: Require less frequent cleaning but still need monitoring for imbalances.

- **Safe disinfectants**: Chlorhexidine or veterinary-safe products are preferred over harsh chemicals.

9.10 Common Mistakes in Substrate and Furnishing Selection

1. **Decor Over Function**
   Choosing items that look attractive but fail to provide functional hiding or climbing spaces.

2. **Unsafe Materials**
   Using sharp rocks, chemically treated wood, or plastics that leach toxins.

3. **Ignoring Species Needs**
   Placing climbing structures for a burrowing

species, or sandy substrates for an arboreal gecko.

4. **Insufficient Hides**
   Providing only one hide, leaving the animal exposed in certain zones.

5. **Unstable Furnishings**
   Loose rocks or branches can fall and injure animals.

9.11 Case Study Examples

- **Leopard Gecko**: Prefers loose sand/clay mixes or paper towels for safety; requires a warm hide, a cool hide, and a moist hide.

- **Green Tree Python**: Needs sturdy horizontal perches for coiling; substrate should support humidity without becoming waterlogged.

- **Tortoises**: Benefit from soil/sand blends for digging and grazing; require shaded hides and flat basking stones.

- **Dart Frogs**: Thrive in bioactive setups with moss, leaf litter, live plants, and climbing structures.

9.12 Aesthetic vs. Functional Balance

While many keepers enjoy designing enclosures as living art pieces, aesthetics should never override animal welfare. A visually stunning terrarium is only successful if it also meets the animal's needs for hydration, temperature regulation, security, and enrichment.

That said, functional naturalistic setups often become aesthetically beautiful as well, as live plants and natural materials create harmony between form and function.

9.13 Conclusion: Building a Home, Not a Cage

Substrates and furnishings are more than decorative choices—they are the foundation of a reptile's or amphibian's daily life. The ground they walk on, the hides they retreat to, and the branches they climb form the landscape of their world.

Providing the right substrate prevents health issues, while thoughtful furnishings reduce stress and encourage natural behaviors. Together, these elements transform captivity into comfort, allowing reptiles and amphibians to not only survive but thrive.

The key lies in **species-specific research, safe material selection, and consistent maintenance**. When keepers build enclosures with these principles in mind, they are not creating cages—they are creating habitats that respect the biology, dignity, and natural heritage of these remarkable animals.

Chapter 10

Handling And Socialization

10.1 Introduction: The Human–Animal Connection

Reptiles and amphibians differ from traditional pets such as dogs or cats in their capacity for social bonding. They are not domesticated species and generally do not seek companionship or affection from humans. Instead, they tolerate interaction to varying degrees, with some species adapting well to handling while others become stressed or even harmed by it.

Despite these differences, handling plays an important role in responsible care. It allows for:

- Routine health checks.

- Gentle acclimation to captivity.

- Stress-free enclosure maintenance.

- Positive human–animal experiences for educational or therapeutic contexts.

The goal of handling and socialization is not to anthropomorphize reptiles and amphibians but to provide safe, respectful interactions that minimize stress and promote wellbeing.

10.2 Understanding Species-Specific Tolerance

Tolerance to handling varies widely across reptiles and amphibians:

- **Generally Tolerant Reptiles**: Bearded dragons, leopard geckos, corn snakes, ball pythons.

- **Moderately Tolerant**: Green iguanas, blue-tongue skinks, red-eared sliders (when out of water).

- **Sensitive or Stress-Prone**: Chameleons, monitor lizards, dart frogs, salamanders.

- **Handling Rarely Appropriate**: Most amphibians, especially delicate frog and salamander species, due to their permeable skin and sensitivity to human oils or chemicals.

Understanding the natural behavior of a species is critical. For example, a prey species that avoids predators by freezing or fleeing may perceive handling as life-threatening, while more sedentary or docile species may adjust over time.

10.3 Preparing for Safe Handling

1. Wash Hands Before and After

- Removes oils, lotions, or contaminants harmful to amphibians.

- Protects keepers from zoonotic bacteria like *Salmonella.*

2. Calm Environment

- Avoid loud noises, sudden movements, or chaotic surroundings.

- Ensure other pets are kept away during handling sessions.

3. Proper Support

- Always support the body fully, especially in long-bodied snakes or heavy lizards.

- Avoid restraining too tightly—animals should feel secure, not trapped.

4. Timing

- Avoid handling during shedding, illness, or right after feeding (to prevent regurgitation).

- Many species are more tolerant of interaction at specific times of day (e.g., crepuscular lizards are calmer during evening hours).

10.4 Handling Techniques

For Lizards

- Approach slowly from the side, not from above (predators attack from above in nature).

- Scoop with both hands, supporting the chest and hindquarters.

- Larger lizards (e.g., iguanas) may require holding the base of the tail to prevent whipping injuries.

For Snakes

- Gently lift from the mid-body, never by the head or tail.

- Use two hands for larger snakes to distribute weight evenly.

- Venomous snakes should never be handled without professional training and proper tools.

For Tortoises and Turtles

- Hold the shell securely with two hands.

- Avoid holding aquatic turtles out of water for long periods—they may overheat or stress.

- Never drop or tip tortoises, as they can injure their spines.

For Amphibians

- Handling should be minimized.

- If necessary, wear clean, wet, powder-free gloves to protect their skin.

- Always keep them moist; never allow prolonged exposure to dry conditions.

10.5 Signs of Stress During Handling

Recognizing body language helps prevent harm.

- **Reptiles**: Hissing, tail whipping, gaping mouths, frantic attempts to escape, darkened coloration.

- **Snakes**: Rapid tongue flicking, musking (releasing foul scent), striking.

- **Amphibians**: Erratic jumping, secretion of toxins from skin, excessive squirming.

If stress signals appear, handling should stop immediately, and the animal should be returned to its enclosure.

10.6 Building Trust and Socialization

While reptiles and amphibians do not bond in the mammalian sense, they can become accustomed to human presence and handling. Strategies include:

- **Short, Frequent Sessions**: Start with just a few minutes and gradually extend.

- **Consistency**: Regular, gentle interactions build familiarity.

- **Positive Associations**: Handle before or after feeding sessions to link human interaction with positive outcomes.

- **Respect Boundaries**: Allow the animal to retreat when it chooses.

Over time, many reptiles will become calm when handled, displaying curiosity rather than fear.

10.7 Special Considerations for Amphibians

Amphibians are especially sensitive to human contact due to:

- **Permeable skin** that absorbs chemicals, salts, and oils.

- **Temperature regulation issues**, as body temperature may shift when held.

- **Moisture loss** during handling.

Because of these vulnerabilities:

- Amphibians should only be handled when absolutely necessary (e.g., for enclosure cleaning, veterinary exams).

- Observational interaction is safer—watching them in naturalistic enclosures provides enrichment without direct contact.

10.8 Handling Frequency and Duration

- **Tolerant reptiles (e.g., bearded dragons, corn snakes)**: Can often be handled several times a week for 10–20 minutes, provided they remain stress-free.

- **Moderate reptiles (e.g., iguanas, skinks)**: Should be handled less frequently to prevent stress.

- **Amphibians**: Handled rarely and only for essential purposes.

It is better to err on the side of **less handling**. Stress can manifest subtly over time, weakening immune systems and shortening lifespans.

10.9 Educational and Therapeutic Handling

Reptiles and amphibians are increasingly used in education and therapy:

- **Educational Programs**: Snakes, lizards, and tortoises help dispel myths and teach biology.

- **Animal-Assisted Therapy**: The calm presence of reptiles can benefit individuals with anxiety or sensory processing needs.

In these contexts:

- Only tolerant, docile individuals should participate.

- Sessions should be short and carefully supervised.

- Hygiene protocols must be strict to protect both animals and humans.

10.10 Hygiene and Safety

For Keepers and Handlers

- Always wash hands with soap and water after handling.

- Avoid touching face, eyes, or mouth before cleaning up.

- Children should be supervised closely when interacting with reptiles or amphibians.

For Animals

- Ensure hands are free of lotions, perfumes, or chemicals.

- Use gloves when handling amphibians or animals with fragile skin.

- Disinfect handling tools (feeding tongs, snake hooks) regularly.

10.11 Common Handling Mistakes

1. **Over-Handling**
   Treating reptiles and amphibians like mammals, expecting them to enjoy prolonged cuddling.

2. **Improper Support**
   Holding snakes by the head or lizards by the tail

leads to injury and stress.

3. **Handling During Vulnerable Times**
   Such as shedding, brumation, or illness.

4. **Allowing Unsafe Exploration**
   Letting reptiles roam unsupervised may lead to injury, escape, or ingestion of harmful objects.

5. **Forcing Interaction**
   Ignoring signs of stress undermines trust and welfare.

10.12 Case Study Examples

- **Bearded Dragon**: With gentle, regular handling, many become calm and will perch comfortably on shoulders.

- **Corn Snake**: Known for their docility, they often tolerate routine handling and are ideal for educational settings.

- **Chameleon**: Typically stress-prone and best observed rather than handled.

- **Dart Frog**: Skin is too delicate for safe handling; observation through glass is the safest interaction.

10.13 Balancing Interaction with Respect

The best keepers recognize that reptiles and amphibians are not domesticated pets designed for constant contact. They are wild animals, even in captivity, and must be treated with respect. Handling should always prioritize the animal's health, safety, and natural behavior over human desire for interaction.

That said, with patience and care, many reptiles learn to tolerate and even seem curious about human presence, making handling a rewarding experience for both keeper and animal.

10.14 Conclusion: Responsible Handling for Welfare

Handling and socialization are essential aspects of reptile and amphibian care, but they must be approached with knowledge, patience, and respect. Proper techniques prevent stress and injury, while consistent, gentle interaction helps animals adjust to human presence.

For reptiles, careful handling enhances husbandry and enriches the human–animal relationship. For amphibians, minimal handling is the key to long-term health.

Ultimately, success lies in understanding each species' tolerance, respecting boundaries, and prioritizing welfare.

When handled responsibly, reptiles and amphibians become not just exotic captives, but ambassadors of their wild counterparts—teaching us to admire, respect, and protect them.

Chapter 11

Health And Common Diseases

11.1 Introduction: The Importance of Health Awareness

Reptiles and amphibians are masters of survival in the wild, often masking illness until it becomes advanced. In captivity, this evolutionary strategy can be fatal if keepers fail to recognize subtle signs of distress. Unlike dogs or cats, these animals rarely vocalize or demonstrate obvious pain, which makes **knowledge of common diseases and early intervention** critical.

Good health care begins with **prevention**: correct diet, proper environmental conditions, clean enclosures, and routine observation. However, even the most carefully maintained animals can fall ill, and keepers must be prepared to identify issues and seek veterinary assistance promptly.

11.2 Recognizing Signs of a Healthy Animal

A healthy reptile or amphibian typically demonstrates:

- **Bright, alert eyes** without discharge.

- **Smooth skin or scales**, free from lesions or unusual discoloration.

- **Regular feeding behavior** appropriate to the species.

- **Normal body posture and movement**, without weakness or paralysis.

- **Well-formed droppings**: feces and urates (in reptiles) should appear consistent and free from blood.

- **Steady weight**: sudden loss is an early sign of illness.

Routine observation is one of the keeper's most powerful tools. Subtle changes in appetite, behavior, or appearance often signal developing health problems.

11.3 Common Health Problems in Reptiles

1. Metabolic Bone Disease (MBD)

- **Cause**: Calcium deficiency, lack of UVB exposure, or incorrect calcium-to-phosphorus ratio.

- **Symptoms**: Soft or deformed bones, tremors, lethargy, difficulty moving or eating.

- **Prevention**: Proper UVB lighting, calcium supplementation, and balanced diet.

2. Respiratory Infections

- **Cause**: Low temperatures, excessive humidity, poor ventilation, or bacterial infection.

- **Symptoms**: Wheezing, open-mouth breathing, nasal discharge, lethargy.

- **Treatment**: Veterinary antibiotics, environmental correction.

3. Parasites

- **Internal parasites** (worms, protozoa) cause diarrhea, weight loss, and weakness.

- **External parasites** (mites, ticks) cause itching, irritation, and anemia.

- **Prevention**: Quarantine new animals, maintain clean enclosures, regular veterinary fecal exams.

4. Shedding Problems (Dysecdysis)

- **Cause**: Low humidity, dehydration, or poor nutrition.

- **Symptoms**: Retained skin, stuck eye caps in snakes, incomplete sheds.

- **Prevention**: Adequate humidity, moist hides, proper hydration.

5. Mouth Rot (Infectious Stomatitis)

- **Cause**: Bacterial infection, often secondary to stress or injury.

- **Symptoms**: Red, swollen mouth, pus or discharge, refusal to eat.

- **Treatment**: Veterinary antibiotics and improved husbandry.

6. Burns

- **Cause**: Direct contact with unshielded heat sources such as heat lamps or hot rocks.

- **Symptoms**: Blisters, necrotic tissue, open wounds.

- **Prevention**: Use thermostats, protective screens, and safe heating methods.

7. Egg Binding (Dystocia)

- **Cause**: Females unable to lay eggs due to poor nutrition, inadequate nesting sites, or oversized eggs.

- **Symptoms**: Restlessness, swelling, straining without producing eggs.

- **Treatment**: Veterinary intervention may involve calcium injections, oxytocin, or surgery.

8. Obesity and Malnutrition

- **Cause**: Overfeeding fatty foods, unbalanced diets, lack of exercise.

- **Symptoms**: Excess fat deposits, lethargy, organ damage.

- **Prevention**: Species-specific diet and proper feeding schedules.

11.4 Common Health Problems in Amphibians

1. Red Leg Syndrome

- **Cause**: Bacterial infection (*Aeromonas* species) linked to poor water quality and stress.

- **Symptoms**: Reddened limbs, lethargy, skin lesions.

- **Treatment**: Antibiotics, strict hygiene, and improved water conditions.

2. Chytridiomycosis

- **Cause**: Fungal infection (*Batrachochytrium dendrobatidis*).

- **Symptoms**: Lethargy, skin thickening, abnormal posture, sudden death.

- **Prevention/Treatment**: Quarantine, antifungal treatments, environmental disinfection. This disease is devastating in wild amphibian populations.

3. Dropsy (Edema)

- **Cause**: Fluid buildup due to kidney failure, infection, or osmotic imbalance.

- **Symptoms**: Swollen body, difficulty moving or floating abnormally.

- **Treatment**: Veterinary care required; supportive treatment may include fluid balance correction.

4. Skin Shedding Issues

- **Cause**: Poor humidity, nutritional deficiencies, fungal infections.

- **Symptoms**: Retained skin, abnormal shedding behavior.

- **Prevention**: Adequate humidity and proper diet.

5. Nutritional Disorders

- **Vitamin A deficiency**: Causes eye swelling, poor vision, and "short tongue syndrome" in frogs.

- **Protein deficiency in tadpoles**: Leads to stunted growth and deformities.

11.5 Preventative Health Care

1. Quarantine New Animals

- Isolate for at least **30–90 days** before introducing to established collections.

- Monitor for parasites, infections, or behavioral abnormalities.

2. Proper Husbandry

- Correct temperatures, humidity, lighting, and enclosure design prevent most diseases.

- Regularly check equipment to ensure consistent conditions.

3. Hygiene and Sanitation

- Daily spot cleaning and regular deep cleaning reduce pathogen buildup.

- Use safe disinfectants such as chlorhexidine or diluted bleach (properly rinsed).

4. Nutrition and Supplements

- Balanced diets with calcium and vitamins prevent nutritional disorders.

- Avoid over-supplementation, which can cause toxicity.

5. Hydration

- Provide clean, dechlorinated water and maintain species-appropriate humidity.

11.6 Routine Health Monitoring

Keepers should develop a habit of daily observation and regular documentation. Key monitoring practices include:

- **Weight checks**: Sudden loss or gain may signal illness.

- **Feeding logs**: Track appetite and feeding behavior.

- **Shedding records**: Identify incomplete sheds.

- **Fecal checks**: Consistency, color, and presence of parasites.

- **Behavioral observation**: Note changes in activity levels or temperament.

A logbook or digital tracking system helps identify gradual changes that may otherwise go unnoticed.

11.7 Veterinary Care for Reptiles and Amphibians

1.   Finding   a   Qualified   Vet
Not all veterinarians are trained in herpetology. Seek an **exotic animal veterinarian** with experience in reptiles and amphibians.

2. Routine Checkups

- Annual exams for healthy animals.

- More frequent visits for breeding animals or those with chronic health conditions.

3. Diagnostic Tools

- Fecal exams for parasites.

- Radiographs (X-rays) for bone health or egg binding.

- Blood tests to assess organ function.

4. **Emergency** **Situations**
Immediate veterinary attention is required for:

- Severe lethargy or collapse.

- Significant weight loss.

- Open wounds or burns.

- Persistent refusal to eat.

- Difficulty breathing.

11.8 Zoonotic Risks and Human Health

Reptiles and amphibians can carry pathogens transmissible to humans:

- **Salmonella**: Common in reptiles; causes gastrointestinal illness in humans.

- **Mycobacteria**: Present in some amphibians and aquatic reptiles.

Prevention includes:

- Hand washing after handling.

- Avoiding reptile or amphibian contact in very young children, elderly individuals, or immunocompromised people.

- Never kissing or eating near reptiles or amphibians.

11.9 Common Mistakes in Health Management

1. **Delaying Veterinary Care**
   Waiting until an animal is severely ill often results in poor outcomes.

2. **Improper Diet**
   Feeding inappropriate foods is one of the leading

causes of preventable illness.

3. **Neglecting Environmental Needs**
    Incorrect humidity or lighting is a major
    contributor to health problems.

4. **Over-Medicating or DIY Treatments**
    Using unverified treatments without veterinary
    guidance may worsen the condition.

5. **Skipping Quarantine**
    Introducing new animals directly into established
    collections spreads parasites and disease.

11.10 Case Study Examples

-   **Metabolic Bone Disease in Bearded Dragons**:
    Preventable with proper UVB and calcium; once
    advanced, often irreversible.

-   **Red Leg Syndrome in Frogs**: Quickly fatal if
    untreated, but preventable with clean water and
    reduced stress.

-   **Parasites in Snakes**: Common in wild-caught
    specimens; routine fecal checks essential.

- **Burns in Tortoises**: Caused by hot rocks or poorly positioned heat lamps.

Each case reinforces the principle that **prevention is easier than treatment**.

11.11 Conclusion: A Proactive Approach to Health

Health care for reptiles and amphibians begins not in the veterinary office, but in the enclosure. Proper husbandry, careful observation, and preventive measures eliminate the vast majority of health problems.

When illness does arise, swift recognition and veterinary consultation are essential. The greatest mistake keepers make is assuming reptiles and amphibians can withstand neglect or recover without care. In truth, their survival depends on attentive, informed keepers who are proactive rather than reactive.

By committing to high standards of health care, keepers not only extend the lives of their animals but also enhance their quality of life, ensuring they thrive as living ambassadors of their wild counterparts.

Chapter 12

Veterinary Care

12.1 Introduction: The Keeper and the Veterinarian

Caring for reptiles and amphibians is a responsibility that goes far beyond feeding and housing. These animals often mask illness until it becomes severe, making professional veterinary support an essential part of responsible ownership. Unlike cats or dogs, reptiles and amphibians require **specialized veterinary knowledge** because their anatomy, physiology, and diseases differ significantly from those of mammals.

Unfortunately, not every veterinarian is trained to treat "exotics," and many keepers delay seeking professional help due to cost, distance, or the misconception that reptiles and amphibians are "hardy" and do not need regular medical attention. In truth, **veterinary care is the cornerstone of long-term health and welfare**, and finding the right vet is as important as choosing the right enclosure or diet.

12.2 The Importance of Exotic Animal Veterinarians

Exotic animal veterinarians (sometimes referred to as "herp vets" when specializing in reptiles and amphibians) have training in:

- Anatomy and physiology unique to ectotherms.

- Diagnostic imaging and laboratory techniques adapted for small or scaled animals.

- Species-specific diseases, parasites, and treatments.

- Husbandry-based illness prevention.

Because reptiles and amphibians often suffer from conditions directly linked to poor husbandry, exotic vets also play the role of **educators**, helping keepers correct errors in lighting, heating, hydration, or diet.

12.3 Routine Veterinary Care

Veterinary care is not only for emergencies—it should be proactive and preventive.

Annual Health Exams

- Even apparently healthy reptiles and amphibians benefit from yearly checkups.

- Exams include weight monitoring, oral inspection, skin and scale checks, and fecal testing for parasites.

- Blood work or X-rays may be recommended for older or breeding animals.

Baseline Health Records

- Establishing normal weight, growth patterns, and blood values for each animal helps detect illness early.

- Keepers should maintain a health log (diet, shedding, weight, fecal output) to share with the vet.

Parasite Screening

- Internal parasites are common in wild-caught specimens and can spread to collections.

- Fecal exams every 6–12 months ensure early detection.

Vaccination

- Unlike mammals, reptiles and amphibians generally do not receive vaccines. Their care focuses instead on prevention through husbandry.

12.4 Emergency Veterinary Care

Because reptiles and amphibians hide symptoms of disease, emergencies often arise suddenly and appear severe. Situations requiring immediate veterinary attention include:

- Severe lethargy or unresponsiveness.

- Open wounds, burns, or fractures.

- Difficulty breathing, gaping, or wheezing.

- Severe bloating, prolapse, or sudden swelling.

- Refusal to eat for prolonged periods (beyond species-specific norms).

- Egg binding in females.

Emergency Preparedness for Keepers

- Identify the nearest exotic vet before an emergency occurs.

- Keep a travel container ready (secure, ventilated, appropriate temperature).

- Maintain a list of emergency contact numbers.

12.5 Diagnostic Tools in Reptile and Amphibian Medicine

Veterinarians employ a range of diagnostic tools adapted for these animals:

- **Physical Exams**: Visual inspection, palpation of body condition, oral and cloacal exams.

- **Radiographs (X-rays)**: Useful for detecting fractures, egg binding, respiratory infections.

- **Ultrasound**: Non-invasive imaging for internal organs, eggs, or tumors.

- **Endoscopy**: Allows visual inspection of internal structures with minimal invasion.

- **Fecal Analysis**: Identifies parasites and digestive health issues.

- **Blood Work**: Assesses organ function and metabolic health.

Because of their small size, amphibians often require specialized micro-sampling techniques.

12.6 Veterinary Treatments

Medication Delivery Methods

- **Oral medications**: Administered via syringe, often mixed with food.

- **Injections**: Intramuscular or subcutaneous; require skill to avoid harming delicate tissues.

- **Topical treatments**: Applied for skin infections or wounds.

- **Bath treatments**: Especially for amphibians— medicated baths deliver drugs through permeable skin.

Surgery in Reptiles and Amphibians

- Performed for egg binding, tumor removal, wound repair, or abscesses.

- Requires specialized anesthesia due to unique respiratory physiology.

12.7 Working with Your Veterinarian

1. Choosing the Right Vet

- Research local clinics and confirm their experience with reptiles and amphibians.

- Seek recommendations from reptile societies, herpetology groups, or zoological facilities.

- Ask about available diagnostic equipment (X-rays, lab testing, endoscopy).

2. Preparing for a Visit

- Transport animals in secure containers with appropriate ventilation.

- Maintain stable temperature during travel using heat packs or insulation.

- Bring a sample of feces, recent health records, and diet information.

3. Communication

- Be honest about husbandry practices, even if errors were made.

- Ask questions and request clarification about diagnoses and treatments.

- Follow instructions carefully regarding medications, dosing, and follow-up visits.

12.8 Preventive Veterinary Partnerships

The most successful reptile and amphibian keepers view veterinary care as a **partnership** rather than a last resort. By working with vets proactively:

- Husbandry issues are corrected before they cause illness.

- Parasites and infections are detected early.

- Breeding animals receive specialized care to ensure reproductive health.

- Keepers gain confidence in recognizing and responding to subtle health changes.

12.9 The Cost of Veterinary Care

Veterinary care for reptiles and amphibians can be expensive due to specialized training and equipment. Common costs include:

- Routine exam: $50–$150.

- Fecal test: $25–$75.

- Blood work: $100–$200.

- Imaging (X-ray, ultrasound): $100–$250.

- Emergency surgery: $300–$1,000+.

Responsible ownership includes planning for these costs through:

- **Emergency funds** set aside for veterinary care.

- **Pet insurance** (some companies now cover exotics).

- Budgeting for annual checkups and preventive tests.

12.10 Common Challenges in Veterinary Care

1. **Lack of Qualified Vets**
    Many regions lack exotic veterinarians, requiring travel or teleconsultation.

2. **Delayed Intervention**
    Keepers often wait too long to seek help, by which time the animal is critically ill.

3. **Self-Medication**
    Using treatments from online sources or pet stores without veterinary supervision can be dangerous.

4. **Transport Stress**
    Travel to clinics can stress animals—proper carriers and temperature control are essential.

12.11 Case Study Examples

- **Egg-Binding in a Green Iguana**: Veterinary intervention with calcium and oxytocin resolved the issue; without care, the animal would have died.

- **Severe Respiratory Infection in a Ball Python**: Prompt antibiotic treatment and husbandry correction saved the snake; delay would have been fatal.

- **Chytridiomycosis in Frogs**: Veterinary antifungal protocols successfully treated the infection, though entire groups were at risk.

- **Burns in a Tortoise**: Surgery and wound care repaired damage caused by a faulty heat lamp.

Each case illustrates that **professional care makes the difference between recovery and decline**.

12.12 Ethics and Responsibility

Veterinary care also intersects with ethical responsibilities:

- **Wild-Caught Animals**: Often carry parasites or stress-related illness; vets can treat them, but keepers should prioritize captive-bred individuals.

- **Euthanasia**: Sometimes the humane choice when illness or injury is irreversible.

- **Preventing Suffering**: Ignoring veterinary care because of cost or inconvenience is unethical.

A responsible keeper ensures every animal in their care has access to proper medical support.

12.13 Conclusion: Veterinary Care as the Backbone of Welfare

Veterinary care is not optional—it is a fundamental requirement of reptile and amphibian husbandry. These animals may appear hardy, but their survival often depends on professional intervention at critical moments.

By forming proactive partnerships with exotic veterinarians, keepers protect their animals against preventable disease, respond effectively to emergencies, and uphold the highest standards of welfare.

A reptile or amphibian may never wag its tail or purr in gratitude, but its health, vitality, and longevity speak volumes. The commitment to veterinary care is the clearest expression of respect and responsibility that any keeper can offer.

Chapter 13

Breeding And Reproduction

13.1 Introduction: Beyond Keeping, Toward Propagation

Breeding reptiles and amphibians is a rewarding yet complex endeavor. It allows keepers to witness the full life cycle of their animals, contribute to conservation efforts, and reduce reliance on wild-caught imports. However, breeding is not simply about producing offspring—it requires **deep biological understanding, precise husbandry, and ethical foresight**.

Reproductive cycles in reptiles and amphibians are strongly influenced by environmental cues such as temperature, photoperiod, humidity, and seasonal changes. Successful breeding replicates these natural conditions while ensuring the health and welfare of both parents and offspring.

13.2 Reasons for Breeding

Conservation

- Many amphibians and some reptiles are threatened by habitat loss and disease. Captive breeding programs help maintain assurance colonies.

Captive-Bred Trade

- Captive breeding reduces demand for wild-caught animals, which often suffer stress, parasites, and high mortality.

Education and Research

- Breeding provides insights into reproductive biology and behavior.

Personal Fulfillment

- Witnessing eggs hatch or tadpoles metamorphose is profoundly rewarding for dedicated keepers.

Caution: Breeding should never be undertaken without a plan for housing or rehoming offspring. Overproduction contributes to neglect and abandonment.

13.3 Basic Biology of Reproduction

Reptiles

- **Oviparous species**: Lay eggs (most lizards, snakes, turtles).

- **Ovoviviparous species**: Retain eggs internally until young hatch (boa constrictors, some skinks).

- **Viviparous species**: Give live birth, nourished by placenta-like structures (some lizards and snakes).

Amphibians

- Typically lay eggs in water or moist environments.

- External fertilization is common in frogs and toads; internal fertilization is more common in salamanders and caecilians.

- Development often includes aquatic larval stages (tadpoles), though some species exhibit direct development (hatch as miniature adults).

13.4 Preparing Adults for Breeding

1. Health Assessment

- Only strong, disease-free adults should be bred. Veterinary exams, fecal tests, and body condition scoring are essential.

2. Age and Size

- Animals must reach maturity; breeding too early leads to health complications. For example, female reptiles bred too young risk egg binding.

3. Nutrition

- Conditioning diets rich in calcium, protein, and vitamins prepare females for egg production and males for spermatogenesis.

4. Seasonal Cycling

- Many species require environmental cues such as brumation (cooling period), rainfall simulation, or daylight shifts to trigger reproductive behavior.

13.5 Courtship and Mating Behaviors

Reptiles and amphibians exhibit fascinating reproductive rituals:

- **Snakes**: Males may engage in combat dances; females release pheromones to attract mates.

- **Lizards**: Visual displays such as head-bobbing, push-ups, or color changes signal readiness.

- **Tortoises**: Males ram or vocalize to court females.

- **Frogs**: Males call to attract females, with each species having distinctive vocalizations.

- **Salamanders**: Courtship often involves pheromone release and tactile signaling.

Keepers must provide adequate space and monitor interactions, as aggression can occur during courtship.

13.6 Nesting and Egg Laying

Reptiles

- Females seek appropriate nesting sites—moist soil, sand, or leaf litter.

- Lack of suitable nesting areas can cause **egg retention (dystocia)**, a life-threatening condition.

- Nest boxes with damp substrates are often required in captivity.

Amphibians

- Frogs and toads deposit eggs in water, often attached to plants.

- Salamanders lay eggs on moist substrates or in water.

- Some species exhibit parental care, guarding eggs or transporting them on their backs.

13.7 Incubation and Development

Reptile Eggs

- Require specific temperature and humidity ranges.

- Incubators with controlled conditions are commonly used.

- Some reptiles exhibit **temperature-dependent sex determination (TSD)**, where incubation temperature determines offspring sex (e.g., many turtles, some lizards).

Amphibian Eggs

- Usually left in water, requiring clean, well-oxygenated conditions.

- Susceptible to fungal infections; antifungal agents or aeration may be needed.

- Tadpoles require careful feeding and water quality management as they grow and metamorphose.

13.8 Live Birth in Reptiles

For viviparous or ovoviviparous species:

- Gestation periods vary from weeks to months.

- Females require stable, stress-free environments during pregnancy.

- Neonates are usually independent at birth but may need smaller enclosures and carefully sized prey.

13.9 Raising Offspring

Reptiles

- Hatchlings should be housed separately or in small groups to prevent cannibalism or competition.

- Enclosures must match species-specific needs but scaled down in size.

- Frequent feeding is necessary due to rapid growth, with appropriate calcium supplementation.

Amphibians

- Tadpoles require algae, specialized feeds, or animal protein depending on species.

- Metamorphosis demands transitioning habitats from aquatic to terrestrial or semi-aquatic setups.

- Juvenile amphibians are often fragile, requiring precise humidity and diet.

13.10 Health Challenges in Breeding

1. **Egg Binding (Dystocia)**

- Particularly common in lizards and snakes if nesting sites or nutrition are inadequate.

2. **Calcium Deficiency**

- Females producing multiple clutches may suffer from depleted calcium stores, leading to metabolic bone disease.

3. **Infections**

- Overcrowding or unsanitary breeding conditions spread parasites and bacterial diseases.

4. **Infertile Eggs**

- Common in inexperienced pairs or poor environmental conditions; infertile eggs may mold or collapse.

5. **High Mortality Rates**

- Especially in amphibians, where delicate eggs and larvae are vulnerable to fungal infections, predation, or poor water quality.

13.11 Ethical Considerations in Breeding

Overproduction

- Flooding markets with common species lowers value, leading to neglect or abandonment.

Inbreeding

- Reduces genetic diversity, causing deformities or reduced fertility. Responsible breeders outcross lines regularly.

Hybridization

- While sometimes producing attractive animals, hybrids may obscure species identity and conservation value.

Wild-Caught vs. Captive-Bred

- Captive breeding should reduce wild collection pressure, not encourage it.

Keeper Responsibility

- Breeding should only be attempted with a plan for housing or rehoming offspring responsibly.

13.12 Conservation Breeding Programs

In zoos and research institutions, breeding is guided by **Species Survival Plans (SSPs)** or similar frameworks. These aim to:

- Preserve genetic diversity.

- Maintain assurance populations of endangered species.

- Develop reintroduction programs.

Private keepers may contribute by responsibly breeding threatened species under proper guidance, though strict regulations often apply.

13.13 Case Study Examples

- **Bearded Dragon Breeding**: Requires brumation, careful nutrition, and nest boxes. Eggs incubated at specific temperatures produce predictable hatching success.

- **Ball Python Breeding**: One of the most successful captive-bred reptiles; temperature cycling and careful pairing lead to viable clutches.

- **Poison Dart Frog Breeding**: Parental care includes males transporting tadpoles to water

pools, requiring highly specialized terrarium
setups.

- **Turtle Breeding**: Temperature-dependent sex
  determination makes controlled incubation
  critical for balanced populations.

13.14 Conclusion: Responsibility Over Curiosity

Breeding reptiles and amphibians is both science and art,
blending biological understanding with environmental
mastery. Yet above all, it is a responsibility. Every egg laid or
tadpole hatched represents a life dependent on the keeper's
knowledge, resources, and ethics.

Done thoughtfully, breeding enriches the lives of keepers,
advances science, and contributes to conservation. Done
carelessly, it leads to suffering, neglect, and ecological harm.

The best breeders are those who ask not, *"Can I breed this
animal?"* but rather, *"Should I?"* and *"Am I prepared to
ensure the welfare of every life I bring into existence?"*

175

Chapter 14

Enrichment And Behavioral Care

14.1 Introduction: Beyond Survival Toward Wellbeing

Historically, reptile and amphibian care focused on the basics—temperature, diet, and enclosure size—ensuring survival rather than wellbeing. Modern husbandry, however, recognizes that these animals are **sentient beings with complex behaviors and instincts**. Meeting their physical needs is not enough; they also require opportunities to express natural behaviors, explore, and adapt.

Enrichment is the practice of enhancing captive environments to stimulate animals mentally and physically. For reptiles and amphibians, this means creating enclosures and routines that encourage climbing, burrowing, hunting, basking, hiding, and even problem-solving. Proper enrichment improves welfare, reduces stress, and allows keepers to witness fascinating behaviors rarely seen in barren setups.

14.2 The Science of Enrichment

Enrichment for reptiles and amphibians draws from animal welfare science, particularly in zoos. Five primary categories are recognized:

1. **Environmental Enrichment**: Modifying enclosures with features that encourage exploration.

2. **Feeding Enrichment**: Offering food in ways that stimulate natural foraging or hunting.

3. **Sensory Enrichment**: Providing new stimuli (visual, tactile, olfactory, auditory).

4. **Cognitive Enrichment**: Challenges that encourage learning or problem-solving.

5. **Social Enrichment**: Opportunities for appropriate interactions, where species-appropriate.

For herpetological species, enrichment must always balance **stimulation with security**. An environment that is too unpredictable may cause stress rather than engagement.

14.3 Understanding Natural Behaviors

To provide meaningful enrichment, keepers must study each species' natural history:

- **Arboreal reptiles** (e.g., chameleons, green tree pythons) need vertical climbing structures and foliage.

- **Burrowing species** (e.g., sand boas, horned frogs) require deep, diggable substrates.

- **Aquatic amphibians** (e.g., axolotls, aquatic frogs) thrive with underwater hides, live plants, and varied flow areas.

- **Active hunters** (e.g., monitors, some snakes) benefit from opportunities to stalk or chase moving prey.

- **Ambush predators** (e.g., ball pythons, pacman frogs) rely on secure hiding spots from which they can ambush food.

The closer captivity mirrors natural ecology, the greater the animal's ability to display authentic behaviors.

14.4 Environmental Enrichment

Climbing Opportunities

- Branches, vines, ledges, and cork bark support arboreal species.

- Textured surfaces encourage natural muscle use and claw health.

Hides and Shelters

- Multiple hiding spots reduce stress by allowing animals to feel secure.

- Warm hides and cool hides let reptiles thermoregulate while concealed.

Digging and Burrowing Substrates

- Sand, soil, coconut fiber, or leaf litter allow digging species to create burrows.

- Amphibians like tiger salamanders thrive with deep, moist substrates.

Water Features

- Shallow pools, waterfalls, or misting systems enhance humidity and hydration.

- Aquatic amphibians benefit from live plants and varying water depths.

Microclimates

- Designing enclosures with temperature and humidity gradients encourages exploration and choice.

14.5 Feeding Enrichment

Live Prey and Hunting

- While controversial in some contexts, live insects and appropriately sized prey encourage natural hunting.

- Prey movement stimulates feeding response and exercise.

Prey Variation

- Rotate feeder insects (crickets, roaches, worms, flies) or offer occasional fish, snails, or greens.

- Variety prevents nutritional deficiencies and boredom.

Food Placement Challenges

- Scatter-feeding insects among foliage.

- Suspend food items to encourage climbing.

- Use feeding puzzles or tubes to mimic foraging.

Target Training

- Teaching animals to associate a visual cue (stick, ball) with feeding promotes controlled interaction.

14.6 Sensory Enrichment

Visual Stimulation

- Moving objects (safe mobiles, fluttering leaves) attract curiosity.

- Changes in enclosure background or décor provide novelty.

Tactile Stimulation

- Rough rocks, smooth logs, moist moss, and varied textures mimic natural landscapes.

- Shallow water baths allow amphibians to hydrate and experience natural tactile input.

Olfactory Enrichment

- Introducing safe scents (herbs, prey odors) stimulates exploratory behavior.

- Rotating décor from other enclosures can introduce new smells.

Auditory Stimulation

- Some amphibians respond to recordings of rainfall or conspecific calls.

- Caution: Loud or continuous noise may stress rather than enrich.

14.7 Cognitive Enrichment

Although often underestimated, reptiles and amphibians show evidence of learning and problem-solving.

- **Obstacle Navigation**: Lizards and turtles can navigate mazes or barriers for food rewards.

- **Target Training**: Crocodilians and large lizards in zoos are trained to station for safe feeding or medical exams.

- **Exploration Opportunities**: Rotating décor and enclosure layouts encourage curiosity and adaptability.

Cognitive enrichment should be challenging but not stressful. Success builds confidence and reduces boredom.

14.8 Social Enrichment

Reptiles and amphibians are generally solitary, but social opportunities may be appropriate in certain contexts:

- **Tortoises** may benefit from group housing if space and resources are abundant.

- **Frogs** like dendrobatids often display natural behaviors in small colonies.

- **Geckos and lizards** may tolerate cohabitation when carefully managed.

Risks of aggression, competition, or disease transmission must always be considered. When in doubt, house individually.

14.9 Seasonal and Environmental Cycling

Enrichment also includes replicating natural seasonal changes:

- **Brumation (winter cooling)**: Necessary for breeding in some reptiles and offers a natural rhythm to life cycles.

- **Rain Simulations**: Trigger breeding behaviors in amphibians and rainforest reptiles.

- **Day/Night Cycles**: Proper photoperiods regulate circadian rhythms and activity.

Cyclical enrichment deepens the animal's connection to natural instincts, even in captivity.

14.10 Monitoring and Evaluating Enrichment

Not all enrichment is beneficial. Keepers must evaluate animal responses:

- **Positive Signs**: Increased activity, exploratory behavior, natural postures, improved feeding.

- **Negative Signs**: Excessive hiding, stress colors, aggression, or refusal to eat.

Rotating enrichment items prevents habituation. Documentation (behavior logs, photos, videos) helps assess long-term impact.

14.11 Health Benefits of Enrichment

- **Physical Fitness**: Climbing, digging, and hunting strengthen muscles and bones.

- **Mental Stimulation**: Reduces stereotypic behaviors such as pacing, glass-surfing, or excessive hiding.

- **Stress Reduction**: Secure hiding places and choice lower chronic stress.

- **Improved Appetite**: Feeding enrichment encourages natural hunting and eating responses.

Animals with enriched environments generally live longer, healthier lives.

14.12 Practical Examples of Enrichment

- **Bearded Dragons**: Rock ledges for basking, scatter-feeding of insects, supervised exploration outside enclosure.

- **Ball Pythons**: Multiple hides, cluttered enclosures with branches, rotating scent trails.

- **Aquatic Frogs**: Live plants, bubble streams, floating cork bark platforms.

- **Box Turtles**: Outdoor enclosures with leaf litter, logs, seasonal fruit scatter-feeding.

- **Dart Frogs**: Complex terrariums with bromeliads, waterfalls, and live insect colonies.

These examples show that enrichment is species-specific but universally beneficial.

14.13 Case Studies

- **Zoo-Housed Komodo Dragon**: Target training and carcass dragging provided mental stimulation and reduced aggression.

- **Captive Dendrobatid Frogs**: Rain simulation and live plant setups triggered courtship and successful egg laying.

- **Corn Snake**: Use of climbing branches and elevated hides increased activity levels and improved body condition.

14.14 Ethical Considerations in Enrichment

Enrichment must prioritize **animal welfare over human entertainment**.

- Avoid unnecessary stress (e.g., excessive handling as "enrichment").

- Ensure novelty does not compromise safety.

- Recognize species-specific needs—what enriches a monitor may overwhelm a dart frog.

14.15 Conclusion: Welfare Through Enrichment

Enrichment transforms captive care from mere survival to genuine welfare. By encouraging natural behaviors and providing stimulating environments, keepers honor the biological heritage of reptiles and amphibians.

The true reward of enrichment is not only healthier animals but also a deeper keeper-animal relationship. Observing a gecko explore a new hide or a frog respond to simulated rain connects us to the wild essence of these creatures.

For reptiles and amphibians, enrichment is not a luxury—it is a necessity, a bridge between captivity and nature, and a daily expression of respect for their complex lives.

Chapter 15

Safety, Ethics, And Responsibility

15.1 Introduction: The Weight of Responsibility

Keeping reptiles and amphibians is both a privilege and a duty. These creatures represent ancient evolutionary lineages, embodying millions of years of adaptation. In captivity, their survival and wellbeing depend entirely on their keepers. Safety, ethics, and responsibility are not optional extras—they are the **foundation of good herpetological husbandry**.

This chapter explores how keepers can safeguard themselves, their animals, and the environment while upholding ethical standards. Responsible care ensures that the hobby contributes positively to conservation, education, and human-animal relationships rather than causing harm.

15.2 Safety for Keepers

1. Handling Precautions

- Always wash hands before and after handling to avoid cross-contamination.

- Use gentle, confident movements; never grab by the tail (can cause injury in lizards).

- Support the animal's body weight fully to reduce stress.

2. Bite and Scratch Risks

- Even non-venomous reptiles can deliver painful bites.

- Turtles may snap unexpectedly; large lizards can scratch with claws.

- Wearing gloves and handling tools minimizes injury risk.

3. Venomous and Dangerous Species

- Venomous snakes, large monitors, and crocodilians should only be kept by highly trained professionals with legal authorization.

- Specialized enclosures, handling equipment (hooks, tongs), and protocols are mandatory.

- Hobbyists are strongly advised against keeping venomous or large predatory reptiles due to the risks involved.

4. Escape Prevention

- Escaped reptiles or amphibians may harm themselves, frighten neighbors, or establish invasive populations.

- Enclosures must be escape-proof, with secure lids, locks, and regular checks for weaknesses.

15.3 Safety for Animals

1. Stress Reduction

- Excessive handling, loud noises, or frequent disturbances cause chronic stress.

- Stress weakens the immune system, making animals more susceptible to illness.

2. Safe Enclosures

- Avoid sharp edges, overheating, or toxic materials.

- All heating elements should be regulated by thermostats and shielded from direct contact.

3. Safe Diet

- Never feed wild-caught insects (may carry pesticides or parasites).

- Avoid inappropriate foods such as dairy, processed meats, or toxic plants.

4. Transportation Safety

- Animals should be transported in secure, ventilated containers with stable temperatures.

- Long journeys require careful planning and monitoring.

15.4 Zoonotic Risks and Human Health

Reptiles and amphibians can transmit diseases to humans, known as **zoonoses**.

- **Salmonella**: The most common, carried by many reptiles. Causes gastrointestinal illness in humans.

- **Mycobacterium species**: Present in aquatic amphibians and reptiles.

- **Parasites**: Can spread through poor hygiene.

Prevention Strategies

- Wash hands thoroughly after handling.

- Do not allow reptiles or amphibians in kitchens or near food preparation areas.

- Avoid contact between vulnerable individuals (infants, elderly, immunocompromised people) and reptiles.

- Teach children proper hygiene and supervision during handling.

15.5 Legal and Regulatory Responsibility

1. Permits and Licensing

- Some species require permits due to conservation status or danger (e.g., venomous snakes, endangered amphibians).

- Ignoring regulations may lead to fines, confiscation, or harm to wild populations.

2. Invasive Species Concerns

- Released or escaped reptiles and amphibians can devastate ecosystems (e.g., Burmese pythons in Florida, cane toads in Australia).

- Responsible keepers never release pets into the wild.

3. International Trade Laws

- The **Convention on International Trade in Endangered Species (CITES)** regulates many reptiles and amphibians.

- Buyers must ensure animals are legally sourced.

15.6 Ethical Dimensions of Herpetoculture

1. Captive-Bred vs. Wild-Caught

- Captive-bred animals are generally healthier, adapt better, and reduce pressure on wild populations.

- Wild-caught individuals often arrive stressed, dehydrated, and parasite-ridden, with high mortality rates.

2. Overbreeding and Overproduction

- Producing more offspring than can be responsibly housed or rehomed contributes to neglect and abandonment.

- Ethical breeders plan ahead and limit breeding to sustainable levels.

3. Species Choice

- Beginners should choose hardy, manageable species rather than difficult or dangerous ones.

- Keeping animals beyond one's skill level is irresponsible and unsafe.

4. Respect for Life

- Reptiles and amphibians deserve the same ethical consideration as mammals.

- Keeping them should never be for novelty or status but for genuine appreciation and stewardship.

15.7 Conservation Responsibility

1. Education and Awareness

- Keepers serve as ambassadors, helping others appreciate reptile and amphibian diversity.

- Public education reduces fear and misinformation, fostering conservation support.

2. Supporting Habitat Protection

- Donating to or volunteering with conservation projects benefits wild populations.

- Responsible keepers value wild habitats as much as captive specimens.

3. Avoiding Exploitation

- The exotic pet trade has contributed to declines in some wild populations.

- Ethical keepers avoid contributing to unsustainable demand.

15.8 Common Ethical Dilemmas

- **Should dangerous species be kept privately?**
  Most argue they should not, due to risks.

- **Is hybridization acceptable?** While it may
  produce unique animals, it can dilute genetic
  integrity.

- **What about euthanasia?** In cases of severe
  suffering or incurable disease, euthanasia is often
  the most humane choice.

- **Is display for entertainment ethical?** Animals
  should be kept primarily for education,
  conservation, or responsible hobby interest—not
  novelty.

15.9 Case Studies

Case 1: Burmese Pythons in Florida
Released or escaped pets have become invasive, preying on
native wildlife and destabilizing ecosystems. This
demonstrates why responsible ownership and escape
prevention are vital.

Case 2: Salmonella Outbreaks from Pet Turtles
In the 1970s, small pet turtles were banned in the U.S. after widespread Salmonella transmission to children. This case highlights zoonotic risk management.

Case 3: Chytrid Fungus and the Amphibian Trade
Global amphibian trade contributed to the spread of chytridiomycosis, a deadly fungal disease. This emphasizes the need for quarantine and biosecurity.

Case 4: Responsible Breeding Programs
Captive breeding of dart frogs has reduced wild collection, demonstrating how ethical breeding supports conservation.

15.10 Keeper's Code of Responsibility

A responsible reptile or amphibian keeper should:

1. Provide proper husbandry (diet, enclosure, temperature, humidity, lighting).

2. Seek veterinary care when needed.

3. Prevent escape or release into the wild.

4. Follow all legal and ethical guidelines.

5. Educate others about responsible care and conservation.

6. Respect the animal as a living being, not a disposable commodity.

15.11 Conclusion: Guardianship, Not Ownership

Keeping reptiles and amphibians is more than a hobby—it is a form of **guardianship**. These creatures depend on humans for survival in captivity, and each decision a keeper makes shapes their quality of life.

Safety ensures that humans and animals coexist without harm. Ethics ensure that care aligns with respect for life and responsibility toward ecosystems. Together, they define the true essence of herpetological stewardship.

In the end, responsible keepers act not as owners but as **guardians of ancient life**, committed to welfare, conservation, and the ethical future of reptiles and amphibians.

Printed in Dunstable, United Kingdom

75839198R00117